100

WORDS

Almost Everyone

Mixes *Up*

OR

Mangles

THE **100** WORDS® *From the Editors of the*
AMERICAN HERITAGE®
DICTIONARIES

HOUGHTON MIFFLIN HARCOURT
Boston New York

EDITORIAL STAFF OF THE

American Heritage® Dictionaries

BRUCE NICHOLS, *Senior Vice President, Publisher, Adult Trade and Reference*

JOSEPH P. PICKETT, *Vice President, Executive Editor*

STEVEN R. KLEINEDLER, *Supervising Editor*

PATRICK TAYLOR, *Senior Lexicographer*

LOUISE E. ROBBINS, *Senior Editor*

SUSAN I. SPITZ, *Senior Editor*

CATHERINE T. PRATT, *Editor*

PETER CHIPMAN, *Associate Editor*

ELIZABETH KASSAB, *Associate Editor*

THE 100 WORDS.® is a registered trademark of Houghton Mifflin Harcourt Publishing Company.

Visit our websites: www.ahdictionary.com
or www.hmhbooks.com

LIBRARY OF CONGRESS CATALOGING-IN-PUBLICATION DATA

100 words almost everyone mixes up or mangles / from the editors of the American Heritage Dictionaries.
    p. cm. -- (The 100 words)
Includes index.
ISBN-13: 978-0-547-39583-8
ISBN-10: 0-547-39583-3
1. English language--Usage--Dictionaries. 2. English language--Errors of usage--Dictionaries. I. Title: One hundred words almost everyone mixes up or mangles.
PE1460.A17 2010
421'.1--dc22

                    2010019039

Text design by George Restrepo

MANUFACTURED IN THE UNITED STATES OF AMERICA

1 2 3 4 5 6 7 8 9 10 - EB - 15 14 13 12 11 10

Table of Contents

100 Words Almost Everyone Mixes Up or Mangles

The 100 Words

Preface

One of the hallmarks of an effective writer is having a command of a sophisticated vocabulary. Good writers know a lot of words, and they know a lot about words. They know which words work in a given situation and which words don't.

Conversely, ineffective writers are notorious for using words incorrectly. They use words in ways that puzzle readers rather than convince them. Many otherwise fine pieces of writing have gone to waste because the writer has shown a poor understanding of a couple of words in key places. Using words in the wrong way, or showing that you are not familiar with certain words that the context clearly requires, is a sure way of undermining the respect of your readers and inviting ridicule.

100 Words Almost Everyone Mixes Up or Mangles highlights some of the most dangerous pitfalls that are scattered throughout the vocabulary of English. The dangers arise from a similarity in sound between two (and sometimes more than two) words. These are words we often hear before we learn how they are spelled. Knowing the differences between these words—and just showing that you are aware that some of these similar-sounding words even exist—can help favorably dispose your readers toward you as a writer and make your point seem thoughtful and well-taken.

What kinds of words are these? Troublesome sound-alikes like *faze* and *phase*, *gibe* and *jibe*, and *hoard* and *horde*. There are also words that sound somewhat alike but have crucial differences in sound and meaning, like *cache* and *cachet*, *delegate* and *relegate*, and *venal* and *venial*. And there are some classic misspellings of well-worn phrases, like *beyond the pail*, *in the throws of,* and *tow the line.* These misspellings arise from a different and erroneous interpretation of the origin of the phrase.

At some time or other, all writers make mistakes like these—they forget that the word *horde* exists, for example, or they think that *cache* means "prestige." Even great writers have stories about their vocabulary blunders. But the stories seem funny only in retrospect.

This book offers you a chance to avoid these embarrassing stories and to develop a more subtle and effective vocabulary. The words are there just waiting to be used. All you have to do is get to know them.

—**Joseph P. Pickett,**
Executive Editor

Guide to the Entries

ENTRY WORDS The 100 words in this book are listed alphabetically. Each boldface entry word is followed by its pronunciation (see page ix for a pronunciation key) and at least one part of speech. One or more definitions are given for each part of speech with the central and most commonly sought sense first.

PART OF SPEECH At least one part of speech follows each entry word. The part of speech tells you the grammatical category that the word belongs to. Parts of speech include *noun, verb, adjective, adverb,* and *preposition.* Some entries are *idioms,* phrases whose meaning is different from the assembled meanings of their individual words.

ORDER OF SENSES Entries having more than one sense are arranged with the central and often the most commonly sought meanings first. In an entry with more than one part of speech, the senses are numbered in separate sequences after each part of speech, as at *cache.*

QUOTATIONS Most words in this book have quotations from books, articles, essays, plays, and speeches that show how the word is used in context. The order of the quotations generally corresponds to the order of senses presented.

ETYMOLOGIES (WORD HISTORIES) Etymologies appear in square brackets following the quotations. An etymology traces the history of a word as far back in time as can be determined with reasonable certainty. The stage most closely preceding Modern English is given first, with each earlier stage following in sequence. A language name, linguistic form (in italics), and brief definition of the form are given for each stage of the derivation presented. For reasons of space, the etymologies sometimes omit certain stages in the derivation of words with long and complex histories, whenever this omission does not significantly detract from a broad understanding of the word's history. To avoid redundancy, a language, form, or definition is not repeated if it is identical to the corresponding item in the immediately preceding stage. The word *from* is used to indicate origin of any kind: by inheritance, borrowing, abbreviation, the addition of affixes, or any other linguistic process. When an etymology splits a compound word into parts, a colon comes after the compound word, and the parts (along with their histories in parentheses) follow in sequence linked by plus signs (+). Occasionally, a form will be given that is not actually preserved in written documents, but that scholars are confident did exist—such a form will be marked by an asterisk (*).

Pronunciation Guide

Pronunciations appear in parentheses after boldface entry words. If a word has more than one pronunciation, the first pronunciation is usually more common than the other, but often they are equally common. Pronunciations are shown after inflections and related words where necessary.

Stress is the relative degree of emphasis that a word's syllables are spoken with. An unmarked syllable has the weakest stress in the word. The strongest, or primary, stress is indicated with a bold mark (ˈ). A lighter mark (ˈ) indicates a secondary level of stress. The stress mark follows the syllable it applies to. Words of one syllable have no stress mark because there is no other stress level that the syllable can be compared to.

The key on page ix shows the pronunciation symbols used in this book. To the right of the symbols are words that show how the symbols are pronounced. The letters whose sound corresponds to the symbols are shown in boldface.

The symbol (ə) is called *schwa*. It represents a vowel with the weakest level of stress in a word. The schwa sound varies slightly according to the vowel it represents or the sounds around it:

a·bun·dant (ə-bŭnˈdənt)   **mo·ment** (mōˈmənt)

civ·il (sĭvˈəl)   **grate·ful** (grātˈfəl)

PRONUNCIATION KEY

Symbol	Examples	Symbol	Examples
ă	pat	oi	noise
ā	pay	o͝o	took
âr	care	o͝or	lure
ä	father	o͞o	boot
b	bib	ou	out
ch	church	p	pop
d	deed, milled	r	roar
ĕ	pet	s	sauce
ē	bee	sh	ship, dish
f	fife, phase,	t	tight, stopped
	rough	th	thin
g	gag	*th*	this
h	hat	ŭ	cut
hw	which	ûr	urge, term,
ĭ	pit		firm, word,
ī	pie, by		heard
îr	deer, pier	v	valve
j	judge	w	with
k	kick, cat, pique	y	yes
l	lid, needle	z	zebra, xylem
m	mum	zh	vision,
n	no, sudden		pleasure,
ng	thing		garage
ŏ	pot	ə	about, item,
ō	toe		edible,
ô	caught,		gallop,
	paw		circus
ôr	core	ər	butter

"So unlike what a man should be!—None of that upright integrity, that strict **adherence** to truth and principle, that disdain of trick and littleness, which a man should display in every transaction of his life."

—Jane Austen, *Emma*

adherence (ăd-hîr′əns)

noun

1. The process or condition of adhering. **2.** Faithful attachment; devotion: *"Adherence to the rule of law . . . is a very important principle"* (William H. Webster).

[From French *adhérence*, from Latin *adhaerentia*, from *adhaerēns, adhaerent-*, present participle of *adhaerēre*, to stick to : *ad-*, to + *haerēre*, to stick.]

∾ In concept at least, *adherence* and *adhesion* both involve the sticking of one thing to another, but *adherence* appears predominantly in figurative contexts while *adhesion* is predominantly physical. So you might describe a glue as having *good adhesion to glass.* But *adherence* is almost never used in this way.

Adherence sees a great variety of nonphysical uses. People can maintain their adherence to the tenets of a religion or philosophy, or demonstrate their adherence to procedure or a set of rules (such as a strict dietary or exercise regimen), but it sounds strange to speak of a person's adhesion to a faith or a diet.

Interestingly, while these two nouns have gone down separate paths, they share the same verb: *adhere.* Mud adheres to your boots, and people adhere to their beliefs.

Scientific evidence exists that atherosclerosis and coronary insufficiency can be reversed by **adherence** to a conscientious program of lifestyle modification involving a strictly vegetarian, low-fat diet, yoga, meditation, group therapy, and moderate exercise.

—Andrew Weil, M.D., *Natural Health, Natural Medicine*

② adhesion (ăd-hē′zhən)

noun

1. The process or condition of sticking or staying attached to a surface. **2.** The physical attraction or joining of two substances, especially the macroscopically observable attraction of dissimilar substances. **3.** A fibrous band of scar tissue that binds together normally separate anatomical structures.

[From French *adhésion,* from Latin a*dhaesiō, adhaesiōn-,* from *adhaesus,* past participle of *adhaerēre,* to adhere; see **adherence** (#1).]

SEE NOTE AT **adherence** (#1).

Her plump upper lip clamped onto the lower as a snail's broad foot clamps onto a leaf, the **adhesion** indicating that she found the topic distasteful and had nothing more to say upon it.

—John Updike, *The Widows of Eastwick*

adopted (ə-dŏp′tĭd)

adjective

1. Having taken on the legal responsibilities as a parent of a child that is not one's biological child. **2.** Having become the owner or caretaker of a pet, especially one from a shelter. **3.** Being a place that one has moved to or resettled in: *one's adopted country.*

[Past participle of *adopt,* from Middle English *adopten,* to adopt, from Old French *adopter,* from Latin *adoptāre* : *ad-,* to, towards + *optāre,* to choose.]

    ~ Children are *adopted* by parents, and we normally refer to an *adopted* child but to *adoptive* parents, families, and homes. When describing places, you can use either *adopted* or *adoptive,* but there is sometimes a slight difference in emphasis. *She enjoys living in her adopted country* emphasizes that she has chosen to live there. *She enjoys living in her adoptive country* suggests that she has adjusted to living there or has been accepted in the community.

 adoptive (ə-dŏp′tĭv)

adjective

1. Characteristic of or having to do with adoption. **2.** Related by adoption: *"increased honesty and sharing between birth families, adoptive families and adoptees"* (Robyn S. Quinter). **3.** Being a place where one has moved or been accepted as a new resident.

[Middle English *adoptif,* from Old French, from Latin *adoptīvus,* from *adoptāre,* to adopt : *ad-,* to, towards + *optāre,* to choose.]

SEE NOTE AT **adopted** (#3).

verb

1. To change something for the better; improve: *We took steps to amend the situation.* **2.** To alter the wording of a legal document, for example, so as to make it more suitable or acceptable. **3.** To enrich soil, especially by mixing in organic matter or sand.

IDIOM:

make amends To make reparations for a grievance or injury caused to someone.

[Middle English *amenden,* to remedy, correct, emend, from Old French *amender,* from Latin *ēmendāre* : *ē-,* variant (used in front of certain consonants) of *ex-,* out + *mendum,* fault.]

✍ *Amend* and *emend* look similar, sound similar, and have similar meanings. In fact, they even come from the same word in Latin. The two words are what linguists call *doublets,* words that derive from the same word in another language, but have taken different forms and meanings because they were borrowed at different times or were affected by an intermediary language (as a Latin word being borrowed through French). *Travel* and *travail,* and *chase* and *catch,* are other examples of doublets.

Etymologically, *amend* and *emend* both mean "to take away a defect or fault," that is, to change something so as to improve it, but each word's range of application is different. When something is amended it is usually improved by an addition or revision, as in the case of the US Constitution, which has been amended by its amendments. Outside of legal contexts, *amend* has fairly broad application. You can amend (that is, correct) someone's remarks, or amend (reform) your life. You can also make *amends* (that is make reparations or compensation) to someone for some offense you have committed. You never make *emends.*

Emend also means to improve, but its range of application is quite narrow. It is used almost solely of texts that are edited or changed. Thus the editors of a literary work emend a text when they suspect that a certain word in it is a mistake, such as one that was miscopied by a scribe copying a manuscript. The editors may emend a word in a line (as in one of Shakespeare's plays) to a different word found in another source, or they may insert a word that they posit must have been intended by the author and was included in the original text, which has been lost.

The noun derived from this verb is *emendation* (not *emendment*).

But the surest sign that his confession had been good and that he had had sincere sorrow for his sin, was, he knew, the amendment of his life.

I have **amended** my life, have I not? he asked himself.

—James Joyce,
A Portrait of the Artist as a Young Man

For the next two weeks she answered the telephone at Women's Services with tight courtesy, hearing but not able to **amend** the sharpness in her manner. The clients who came in asked to talk to other counselors.

—Erin McGraw, *The Good Life*

 **baleful** (bāl′fəl)

adjective

1. Portending evil; ominous: *The guard's baleful glare frightened the children.* **2.** Harmful or malignant in intent or effect: *a baleful influence.*

[Middle English, from Old English *bealoful* : *bealu,* harm, injury + *full,* full.]

   ∾ *Baleful* and *baneful* have pretty much the same meanings, but *baneful* most often describes that which is actually harmful or destructive, and it frequently modifies words such as *effects, consequences,* and *influence.*
     Like *baneful, baleful* is used to characterize harmful effects and influences, but it is most often applied to something that is menacing or that foreshadows evil, so the range of words it modifies tends to be broader.

Speak, Winchester; for boiling choler chokes
The hollow passage of my poison'd voice,
By sight of these our **baleful** enemies.

—William Shakespeare,
Henry VI , *Part I:* Act 5, Scene 4, 120–122

Her temper was too sweet for her to show any anger, but she felt that her happiness had received a bruise, and for several days merely to look at Fred made her cry a little as if he were the subject of some **baleful** prophecy.

—George Eliot, *Middlemarch*

The **baleful** presence of Babe Ruth also seemed to throw a scare into Gharrity, the Senator's catcher.

—Glenn Stout, *Top of the Heap: A Yankees Collection*

There on the great high-backed carved oak chair by the right side of the fire-place sat an enormous rat, steadily glaring at him with **baleful** eyes. He made a motion to it as if to hunt it away, but it did not stir. Then he made the motion of throwing something. Still it did not stir, but showed its great white teeth angrily, and its cruel eyes shone in the lamplight with an added vindictiveness.

—Bram Stoker, *Dracula's Guest*

7 baneful (bān′fəl)

adjective

1. Causing harm, ruin, or death; harmful: *the baneful effects of the poison.* **2.** Portending harm; ominous: *a baneful dream.*

[Compound of *bane,* harm, ruin, death (from Middle English, from Old English *bana*) + *-ful,* full (from Middle English, from Old English *–full*).]

SEE NOTE AT **baleful** (#6).

In due course, the Committee found that Keynes was, indeed, exerting a **baneful** influence on the Harvard economic mind and that the Department of Economics was unbalanced in his favor.

—John Kenneth Galbraith,
"How Keynes Came to America,"
Economics, Peace and Laughter

Then I sat down in a pink straight-backed wicker chair at an oaken desk, also painted pink, whose coarse-grained and sturdy construction reminded me of the desks used by schoolmarms in the grammar-school classrooms of my childhood, and with a pencil between thumb and forefinger confronted the first page of the yellow legal pad, its barrenness **baneful** to my eye.

—William Styron, *Sophie's Choice*

---

8 beyond the pale

idiom

Utterly unacceptable or unreasonable.

[After the *Pale*, the medieval dominions of the English in Ireland, from Middle English *pale,* stake, picket, from Old French *pal,* from Latin *pālus.*]

∽ A good way to remember the proper spelling of an expression is to know its origin. In the case of *beyond the pale,* pails and buckets are not part of the story, nor is the adjective *pale* that means "of light hue," as in *pale yellow.* The *pale* of *beyond the pale* is related to the word *pole* and refers to a pointed stake or picket. Such stakes are commonly used to fence in or simply mark the boundaries of pieces of land. As early as the 1300s, the word *pale* came to be used for the boundary or fence itself; by 1400 it was applied to the land inside the boundary.

In the 1500s, the word developed into a proper noun. People within *the English Pale* or *the Pale* were subject to English jurisdiction and protection; lands beyond the Pale were considered by the English to be hostile and dangerous.

Today, the expression is used metaphorically and means "outside of the limits of acceptability." Note that the word *pale* is not capitalized when the expression is used in this way.

"You think . . . about the scene you had with him in front of her. You think this might be the best way of explaining to her how it's happened that you've left him. You want to explain that you of all women don't have to take whatever your husband gives you. That some things are simply **beyond the pale.**"

—Jonathan Franzen, *The Twenty-Seventh City*

9 cache (kăsh)

noun

1. An amount of goods or valuables, especially when kept in a concealed or hard-to-reach place: *They maintained a cache of food in case of emergencies.* **2.** The concealed or hard-to-reach place used for storing a cache.

verb

To hide or store something in a cache.

[French, from *cacher,* to hide, from Old French, to press, hide, from Vulgar Latin **coācticāre,* to store, pack together, from Latin *coāctāre,* to constrain, from *coāctus,* past participle of *cōgere,* to drive (cattle) together, pack together, constrain : *co-,* together + *agere,* to drive.]

ↆ Both *cache* and *cachet* come from French, and they are sometimes confused. *Cache,* meaning "a store of goods stashed in a hiding place," began to appear frequently in English in the early 19th century. Thus, the police might find a cache of drugs or a cache of stolen money hidden at a crime scene, or a group of explorers might hide a cache of supplies to be used on their return trip. It is properly pronounced like the word *cash.* (Note that there is no accent mark over the *e.*) The word is sometimes pronounced with two syllables as (kă-shā**′**), but this pronunciation is not considered standard and may be viewed as a mistake by people who know French.

Cachet means "a mark of distinction, prestige." It originally referred to a seal that closed letters and identified the writer, who was often an important person or aristocrat. Nowadays a prestigious university might attract students because it *has cachet,* or a certain brand of product might be popular because it *has a certain cachet. Cachet* is pronounced with two syllables: (kă-shā**′**). When spelling this word, people sometimes mistakenly leave off the final *–t.*

He opened the bottom desk drawer, where he was hoping to store the tax returns, and came upon a **cache** of sickroom supplies.

—Anne Tyler, *Digging to America*

They looked then for the cave where the robbers might have **cached** banknotes and bars of gold.

—Annie Proulx, "The Governors of Wyoming,"
Close Range: Wyoming Stories

10 cachet (kă-shā′)

noun

1a. A mark or quality, as of distinction, individuality, or authenticity: *"Federal courts have a certain cachet which state courts lack" (Christian Science Monitor).* **b.** Great prestige or appeal: *a designer label with cachet.* **2.** A seal on a document, such as a letter.

[French *cachet*, small seal, impression left by a seal, distinctive character, from Old French, small seal, from *cacher*, to press; see **cache** (#9).]

SEE NOTE AT **cache** (#9).

Because it could be easily carved, ivory in the nineteenth century was a more rare and expensive version of what plastic is today, with the added **cachet** of having an exotic origin—a **cachet** that grew greater with the public idolization of African explorers.

—Adam Hochschild, *King Leopold's Ghost*

11 condemn (kən-dĕm′)

verb

1. To express strong disapproval of: *condemned the needless waste of food.* **2.** To pronounce judgment against; sentence: *condemned the felons to prison.* **3.** To judge or declare to be unfit for use or consumption, usually by official order: *condemn an old building.* **4.** To force someone to experience, endure, or do something: *"No art critic likes to be condemned to a steady diet of second-rate stuff"* (Ben Ray Redman).

[Middle English *condemnen*, from Old French *condemner*, from Latin *condemnāre* : *com-*, together (also used as an intensive prefix) + *damnāre,* to sentence (from *damnum,* penalty).]

∾ *Condemn* and *contemn* both involve the expression of disapproval, but there is a significant difference between the two. *Condemn* often means "to express strong disapproval of, declare unfit," as in *The inspector condemned the lack of safety precautions.* It also means "to pronounce judgment against; sentence," as in *The judge condemned the felon to prison.* By extension it means "to force someone to do or endure something," as in George Santayana's famous maxim "Those who cannot remember the past are condemned to repeat it." In origin, *condemn* is related to *damnation.* Both words derive from Latin *damnum,* meaning "injury, damage," and also "legal penalty."

Contemn, on the other hand, means "to despise, hold in contempt." In the sentence *He contemned the wasteful society in which he lived, contemn* simply describes the subject's attitude of scorn, whereas in the sentence *He condemned the wasteful society in which he lived, condemn* suggests that he voiced his disapproval openly or came to a realization of something he had only vaguely understood before. The verb *contemn* is also found in legal writing with the technical meaning "to display open disrespect or willful disobedience of the authority of a court of law or legislative body." (*Contemner* or *contemnor,* the agent noun formed from *contemn,* is sometimes found in the meaning "a person held in contempt of court.") *Contemn* is the verb corresponding to the noun *contempt*, and both words are ultimately derived from the Latin verb *contemnere*, "to despise, disdain."

Contemn can furnish a useful if rather literary synonym for *despise*. Although the word can sound somewhat stiff and artificial today, it has an illustrious pedigree in English. Shakespeare used it on several occasions, and the translators of the King James Version of the Bible chose *contemn* almost a dozen times in rendering words meaning "scorn," as in *Because they rebelled against the words of God, and contemned the counsel of the most High: Therefore he brought down their heart with labour* (Psalms 107:11–12).

For years I had **condemned** her as a woman without heart, who loved merely power over men and the momentary satisfaction to vanity or flesh which they could give her, who lived in a strange, loveless oscillation between calculation and instinct.

—Robert Penn Warren, *All the King's Men*

Her heart sympathized in the rebellion against his father's commands, which her brother had confessed to her in an unusual moment of confidence, but her uneasy conscience **condemned** the deceit which he had practised.

—Elizabeth Gaskell, *Ruth*

His second wife, Helen's mother, was younger by twenty years, a spirited woman of intellect **condemned** to farmhouse toil.

—Cynthia Ozick, "What Helen Keller Saw," *The Din in the Head adjective*

1. Of or relating to a condition that is present at birth, as a result of either heredity or environmental influences: *a congenital heart defect; congenital syphilis.* **2.** Being or having an essential characteristic as if by nature; inherent or inveterate: *"the congenital American optimism that denies conflicts and imagines all stories having happy endings"* (Robert J. Samuelson).

[From Latin *congenitus,* congenital : *com-,* together, jointly + *genitus,* born, past participle of *gignere,* to bear.]

∾ The words *congenital* and *inherited* both refer to diseases or conditions that exist at birth. Abnormal characteristics or conditions that are *inherited* are a result of genetic or chromosomal defects, as in hemophilia. Inherited diseases are also called *genetic* diseases. The signs of disease may be present at birth, as in Down syndrome, or they may not appear until later in life, as in Huntington's disease. The word *congenital* is derived from the Latin *com-,* meaning "together," and *genitus,* meaning "born." Although all inherited diseases are technically congenital, not all congenital conditions are inherited.

The word *congenital* is most often used to describe what are called *congenital anomalies,* or structural defects present at birth. These conditions may be inherited, or they may result from toxic factors in the prenatal environment, such as drugs, chemicals, infections, radiation, poor nutrition, or traumatic injuries, as from oxygen deprivation. The defect may be apparent, as in congenital deafness or dwarfism, or microscopic. Sometimes it is not known whether a congenital defect is a result of an inherited mutation or environmental influences, as in many kinds of congenital heart disease. *Congenital* is also often used to describe conditions resulting from trauma during labor or delivery, such as cerebral palsy.

Unlike the word *inherited, congenital* sometimes sees figurative use meaning "habitual" or "inveterate."

13 contemn (kən-tĕm′)

verb

To view with contempt; despise.

[Middle English *contempnen,* to slight, spurn, from Latin *contemnere,* to despise : *com-,* together (also used as an intensive prefix) + *temnere,* to despise.]

SEE NOTE AT **condemn** (#11).

In the case of a pope as controversial as John Paul II, biographers are likely either to venerate him as the embodiment of Catholicism or **contemn** him as its corrupter.

—Christopher Caldwell, "'Universal Father' and 'The Pontiff in Winter': The Loneliest Job," *New York Times,* May 15, 2005

14 contemptible (kən-tĕmp′tə-bəl)

adjective

Deserving of contempt; despicable.

[Middle English, from Latin *contemptibilis,* from *contemptus,* past participle of *contemnere,* to despise; see **contemn** (#13).]

∽ *Contemptible* and *contemptuous* are both useful words that can sometimes be confusing, but it is not difficult to keep them separate. *Contemptible* means "deserving of contempt, despicable." It leads a healthy existence in denunciations of all kinds but also has led a distinguished life in literature.

Contemptuous means "manifesting or feeling contempt; scornful." The word is often followed by the preposition *of.*

As a general principle and abstract proposition, Miggs held the male sex to be utterly **contemptible** and unworthy of notice; to be fickle, false, base, sottish, inclined to perjury, and wholly undeserving.

—Charles Dickens, *Barnaby Rudge*

"Never mind, Harriet, I shall not be a poor old maid; and it is poverty only which makes celibacy **contemptible** to a generous public!"

—Jane Austen, *Emma*

15 **contemptuous** (kən-tĕmp′chōo-əs)

adjective

Manifesting or feeling contempt; scornful.

[From Latin *contemptus* (stem *contemptu-*), contempt, from *contemptus*, past participle of *contemnere*, to despise; see **contemn** (#13) + *-ous*, adjective suffix (from Middle English, from Old French *-ous*, *-eus*, *-eux*, from Latin *-ōsus* and *-us*, adjective suffixes).]

SEE NOTE AT **contemptible** (#14).

Anyone who had looked at him as the red light shone upon his pale face, strange straining eyes, and meagre form, would perhaps have understood the mixture of **contemptuous** pity, dread, and suspicion with which he was regarded by his neighbours in Raveloe.

—George Eliot, *Silas Marner*

Contemptuous of all his own underlings, politicians, generals, and diplomats alike, Stalin showed himself impressed by his alliance partners; they were men of power and destiny, whom he considered to be of his own stature in history.

—Peter Grose, *Operation Rollback: America's Secret War Behind the Iron Curtain*

All in all Beatrice O'Hara absorbed the sort of education that will be quite impossible ever again; a tutelage measured by the number of things and people one could be **contemptuous** of and charming about; a culture rich in all arts and traditions, barren of all ideas, in the last of those days when the great gardener clipped the inferior roses to produce one perfect bud.

—F. Scott Fitzgerald, *This Side of Paradise*

delegate (dĕl′ĭ-gāt′)

verb

1. To authorize and send another person as one's representative. **2.** To commit or entrust a task or responsibility to another.

[From Latin *dēlēgāre* (with past participle *dēlēgātus*), to delegate, dispatch : Latin *dē-*, from, away, down + Latin *lēgāre*, to delegate (from earlier "to commission by contract," from *lēx, lēg-*, law).]

SEE NOTE AT **relegate** (#74).

[Mayor Maynard] Jackson asked Reagan for a meeting to discuss the crisis in Atlanta. Reagan **delegated** his vice president, George Bush, to communicate with Jackson.
—Bernard Headley, *The Atlanta Youth Murders and the Politics of Race*

Child care may be **delegated** to others to the point that neither parent is primary in the child's upbringing.
—Judith S. Wallerstein and Sandra Blakeslee, *The Good Marriage: How and Why Love Lasts*

In the past, most food that children consumed was prepared by people who knew and loved them. Now we have **delegated** this fundamental responsibility to strangers whose primary consideration is profit, not our health.
—David Ludwig, M.D., *Ending the Food Fight*

17 **deprecate** (dĕp′rĭ-kāt′)

verb

1. To belittle or disparage; depreciate. **2.** To express strong disapproval of; deplore or condemn.

[Latin *dēprecārī* (with past participle *dēprecātus),* to ward off by prayer : *dē-,* from, away, down + *precārī,* to pray (from *precēs,* prayers).]

∾ Like many words, the verb *deprecate* has seen some changes in meaning over its history. It originally meant "to pray in order to ward off something, ward off by prayer." Perhaps because the occasion of such prayers was invariably one of dread, the word developed the more general meaning of disapproval, as in this well-known quotation from Frederick Douglass: *"Those who profess to favor freedom, yet deprecate agitation, are men who want crops without plowing up the ground."* From here it was a small step to add the meaning "to make little of, disparage," what was once the proper meaning of *depreciate.* This sense of *deprecate* has become the most common one, with the meaning of "deplore" fading and becoming old-fashioned. This trend is probably being encouraged by the widespread use of the adjective *self-deprecating* as a synonym for *modest.*

By contrast, the traditional "disparage" meaning of *depreciate* appears to be getting crowded out by the word's abundant use in the world of finance, where it means "to diminish (or cause to diminish) in price or value," as in *Our car has depreciated in value* and *Their savings was depreciated by inflation.* The word sometimes gets extended to nonmonetary kinds of value, as in an act that depreciates someone's estimation in the eyes of others.

So with these two words we are witnessing a change in progress. While *deprecate* and *depreciate* still share the meaning "to belittle," the words are slowly going their separate ways, with *deprecate* becoming sole owner of the "belittlement" meaning, and *depreciate* primarily used to indicate a lowering in value.

I was covered with a strong flush which is the radiance an older fellow may allowably feel after such a victory. But I

---

tried to **deprecate** the whole thing and said to him, "I have experience on my side. You'll never know how much and what kind."

—Saul Bellow, *Henderson the Rain King*

To those who believe we are likely to experience a common portion of the vicissitudes and calamities which have fallen to the lot of other nations, they must appear entitled to serious attention. Such men must behold the actual situation of their country with painful solicitude, and **deprecate** the evils which ambition or revenge might, with too much facility, inflict upon it.

—Alexander Hamilton, "Federalist No. 30," December 28, 1787

18 **depreciate** (dĭ-prē′shē-āt′)

verb

1. To lessen or diminish in price or value: *An increase in the supply of money depreciated the country's currency.* **2.** To think or speak of as being of little worth; belittle.

[Medieval Latin *dēpreciāre* (with past participle stem *dēpreciāt-*), to lower the value of, alteration of Latin *dēpretiāre* : *dē-*, from, away, down + *pretium*, price.]

SEE NOTE AT **deprecate** (#17).

They took out a subprime mortgage for $280,000, but their house has **depreciated** to a value today of $200,000.

—John D. Geanakoplos and Susan P. Koniak, "Matters of Principal," *New York Times*, March 4, 2009

Dubin, raising his voice, accused her of having **depreciated** his love for her.

—Bernard Malamud, *Dubin's Lives*

19 **distinct** (dĭ-stĭngkt′)

adjective

1. Readily distinguishable from all others; discrete: *on two distinct occasions.* **2.** Easily perceived by the senses: *a distinct flavor.* **3.** Clearly defined; unquestionable: *at a distinct disadvantage.*

[Middle English, from Latin *distīnctus,* from past participle of *distinguere,* to distinguish; see **distinctive** (#20).]

   ~ Because something that serves to identify is often readily distinguishable, *distinct* and *distinctive* are sometimes used in the same ways, but each word imparts a different emphasis.

    A thing is *distinct* if it is sharply distinguished from other things; a property or attribute is *distinctive* if it enables us to distinguish one thing from another. *There are two distinct colors on the face of the Canada goose* means that the two colors are clearly different from each other, while *There are two distinctive colors on the face of the Canada goose* means that the two colors are different from colors found on the faces of other birds, and the Canada goose may be identified by these two colors.

    Sometimes a thing can be both distinct and distinctive. *An infant with a distinct personality* has a personality that one can distinguish from the personalities of other infants. *An infant with a distinctive personality* has a personality that is unique to it and serves to identify it.

It may be asked, how is it that varieties, which I have called incipient species, become ultimately converted into good and **distinct** species, which in most cases obviously differ from each other far more than do the varieties of the same species? How do those groups of species, which constitute what are called **distinct** genera, and which differ from each other more than do the species of the same genus, arise?

—Charles Darwin, *On the Origin of Species*

They could feel each step as a **distinct** vibration now—two ten-ton animals, moving toward them.

—Michael Crichton, *The Lost World*

Leopold had a **distinct** tendency to fall off horses and no visible sense of humor. He was an ungainly, haughty young man whom his first cousin Queen Victoria of England thought "very odd" and in the habit of "saying disagreeable things to people."

—Adam Hochschild, *King Leopold's Ghost*

20 **distinctive** (dĭ-stĭngk′tĭv)

adjective

1. Serving to identify; distinguishing or characteristic: *the distinctive call of the hermit thrush.* **2.** Distinguished or attractive: *The new table gave the room a distinctive appearance.*

[Latin *distīnct-*, stem of *distīnctus*, past participle of *distinguere*, to distinguish + English *-ive*, adjective suffix (from Middle English, from Old French, from Latin *–īvus*).]

SEE NOTE AT **distinct** (#19).

She writes and illustrates children's books, all of them about a family of goats who are given **distinctive** individual features like reading glasses, **distinctive** smirks, uncombed forelocks, and scowls that Lydia has picked up from her two ex-husbands and her own children.

—Charles Baxter, *The Feast of Love*

Her forefinger tracked the cleft in his chin, and she thought how **distinctive** it made him look.

—Joan Johnston, *Texas Woman*

21 **emend** (ĭ-měnd′)

verb

To improve a text or line of text by critical editing.

[Middle English *emenden*, from Latin *ēmendāre* : *ē-*, *ex-*, out of, away from + *mendum*, defect, fault.]

SEE NOTE AT **amend** (#5).

The base-text for this **emended** edition is the carbon-copy typescript of *O Lost* typed from Thomas Wolfe's manuscript. This published text has been established by collation of the carbon copy against the manuscript to identify and **emend** the typist's misreadings.
>   —Matthew J. Bruccoli, Introduction to *O Lost:*
>   *A Story of the Buried Life* by Thomas Wolfe,
>   edited by Arlyn and Matthew J. Bruccoli

For two centuries editors have agreed that the second line [of the speech by Macbeth] is unsatisfactory and have **emended** "no" to "do": "Who dares do more is none."
>   —Sylvan Barnet, Introduction to his edition of
>   *Macbeth* by William Shakespeare

22 **energize** (ĕn′ər-jīz′)

verb

1. To give energy to; activate or invigorate. **2.** To supply with an electric current.

[From *energy* (from French *énergie*, from Late Latin *energīa*, from Greek *energeia*, from *energos*, active : *en-*, in, at + *ergon*, work) + *-ize*, verb suffix (from Middle English *-isen*, from Old French *-iser*, from Late Latin *-izāre*, from Greek *–izein*).]

SEE NOTE AT **enervate** (#23).

They all watched as she hurried from the room, but no one questioned her, such was the general fatigue. She, on the other hand, was taking the stairs two at a time, **energized** now by a sense of doing and being good, on the point of springing a surprise that could only earn her praise.

—Ian McEwan, *Atonement*

The nearest SAM-equipped ship, the frigate Groves, immediately **energized** her missile radars and fired a surface-to-air missile at the oncoming Bear.

—Tom Clancy, *Red Storm Rising*

23 **enervate** (ĕn′ər-vāt′)

verb

To weaken or destroy the strength or vitality of someone or something.

[Latin *ēnervāre* (with stem *ēnervāt-*), to cut the sinews of (a person or animal), enervate : *ē-*, *ex-*, out of, away from + *nervus*, sinew.]

∾ Sometimes people mistakenly use the verb *enervate* to mean "to invigorate" or "to excite" by assuming that this word is a close cousin of the verb *energize*. In fact *enervate* means the opposite of *energize*, and the words come from different sources. *Energize* comes from the Greek word *energos*, meaning "active," whereas *enervate* comes from Latin *nervus*, "sinew." By etymology at least, *enervate* means "to cause to become out of muscle," that is, "to weaken or deplete of strength or vigor."

Enervate is often used as a participial adjective: *enervating* or *enervated*.

But why do men degenerate ever? What makes families run out? What is the nature of the luxury which **enervates** and destroys nations?

—Henry David Thoreau, *Walden*

That goal seemed to invigorate the United States and **enervate** El Salvador, which had dominated play for more than an hour, urged on by a loud and passionate crowd.

—Paul Oberjuerge, "U.S. Grabs Late Goals and Tie in El Salvador," *New York Times*, March 29, 2009

24 exceptionable (ĭk-sĕp′shə-nə-bəl)

adjective

Open or liable to objection or disapproval.

[From *exception* (from Old French, from Latin *exceptiō*, stem *exceptiōn-*, from *exceptus*, past participle of *excipere*, to exclude : *ex-*, out of, away from + *capere*, to take) + *-able*, adjective suffix (from Middle English, from Old French, from Latin *–ābilis*).]

～ While *exceptionable* does not see frequent use today, it is sometimes used incorrectly for *exceptional*. These two words look similar but have very different meanings. *Exceptionable* has a negative meaning, and *exceptional* usually has a positive one. Only *exceptionable* means "objectionable" or "causing disapproval": *The teachers were relieved to find nothing exceptionable in the student newspaper*. *Exceptional* means "uncommon" or "extraordinary." When *exceptional* means "uncommon" or "being the exception to the rule," as it were, it can sometimes occur in negative contexts and be confused with *exceptionable*.

> "We can't have perfection; and if I keep him, I must sustain his administration as a *whole*, even if there are, now and then, things that are **exceptionable**."
>
> —Harriet Beecher Stowe, *Uncle Tom's Cabin*

> The letter was of a partisan character; wholly unbecoming the commander-in-chief of the army, and highly **exceptionable** in its tenor and language towards the President.
>
> —James K. Polk, *The Diary of James K. Polk During His Presidency, 1845 to 1849*

(25) exceptional (ĭk-sĕp′shə-nəl)

adjective

1. Being the exception; uncommon: *Our town is exceptional for the region in having a high tax rate.* **2.** Well above average; extraordinary: *an exceptional memory.* **3.** Deviating widely from a norm, as of physical or mental ability: *special educational provisions for exceptional children.*

[From *exception* (from Old French, from Latin *exceptiō* (stem *exceptiōn-*), from *exceptus,* past participle of *excipere,* to exclude : *ex-,* out of, away from + *capere,* to take) + *-al,* adjective suffix (from Middle English, from Old French, from Latin *-ālis,* adjective suffix).]

SEE NOTE AT **exceptionable** (#24).

The most unmistakable chemical transformation is that of a matter's state—a solid liquefies, a liquid evaporates, a vapor condenses into rain. For most of the furnishings of our everyday life, we associate a particular substance with only one of those three states. . . . Water again bucks convention and seems almost equally at home in all three forms, as ice, steam, and liquid. In fact, Earth is **exceptional** in its possession of tristate water. Mars has a lot of water, but it's frozen away underground. Jupiter and Saturn have traces of water, too, but as orbiting ice crystals or as a gas among miasmic gases. Only on Earth are there ocean flows and Arctic floes and sputtering Yellowstone fumaroles; only the Goldilocks planet has water to suit every bear.

—Natalie Angier, *The Canon: A Whirligig Tour of the Beautiful Basics of Science*

When Nancy was thirteen she'd placed second in a race at her all-girls school, a run of about two miles, and she saw the possibility of something in which she could be **exceptional**. She was good in everything else, but this was another kind of stardom.

—Philip Roth, *Everyman*

But so familiar was Yangon in its sameness and its smells that I easily found my way around. . . . Apart from the newly painted pagodas, the city was ruinous, which was unique in the reinvented Southeast Asia. Myanmar was **exceptional** in its decrepitude and low morale, its inefficiency almost total.

—Paul Theroux, *Ghost Train to the Eastern Star*

26 **expedient** (ĭk-spē′dē-ənt)

adjective

1. Suitable or efficient for accomplishing a purpose: *We all thought email was the most expedient way to communicate with our distant relatives.* **2.** Convenient but based on a concern for self-interest rather than principle: *My opponent often changes his position when it is politically expedient.*

noun

1. Something that is a means to an end, especially when based on self-interest: *She compromises only as an expedient to boost her career.* **2.** Something contrived or used to meet an urgent need: *They really exhausted every expedient before filing the lawsuit.*

[Middle English, from Latin *expediēns, expedient-,* present participle of *expedīre,* to disentangle, extricate, prepare for use (originally, "to release from a snare"): *ex-,* out of, away from + *pēs, ped-,* foot.]

    ↶ *Expedient* and *expeditious* can sometimes be confused. Something that is *expedient* is appropriate to a specific purpose, but may not be ethically or morally appropriate. For instance, you might take an expedient course of action to get a job done, but if you are friendly only when friendliness is expedient to getting that job done, your expedient friendliness is dishonest. The similar-looking word *expeditious* is more straightforward: an action that is expeditious is an action done with speed and efficiency.

Had she not gone out of her way to bury old hatchets and show these people that she bore them no ill will for their gossiping and backbiting? Surely they must know that she didn't like Governor Bullock any more than they did but that it was **expedient** to be nice to him.

—Margaret Mitchell, *Gone with the Wind*

27 **expeditious** (ĕk′spĭ-dĭsh′əs)

adjective

Acting or done with speed and efficiency.

[Latin *expedīre, expedīt-,* to disentangle, extricate, make ready (originally, "to release from a snare," from *ex-,* out of, away from + *pēs, ped-,* foot) + *-ous,* adjective suffix (from Middle English, partly from Latin *-ius* and partly from Old French *-ieus, -ieux,* from Latin *-iōsus*).]

SEE NOTE AT **expedient** (#26).

But I kept my own counsel, and I did my work. I knew from the first that, if I could not do my work as well as any of the rest, I could not hold myself above slight and contempt. I soon became at least as **expeditious** and as skillful as either of the other boys.

—Charles Dickens, *David Copperfield*

In truth he was already reveling in the promise of the reward and celebrity that his **expeditious** capture of this villain would bring.

—Anne Perry, *Much Ado About Murder*

How, they must surely be asking themselves, had he found time to make so many inquiries? Or would they merely put it all down to the **expeditious** methods of our county police?

—Ngaio Marsh, *Clutch of Constables*

 **faze** (fāz)

verb

To disrupt the composure of someone; disconcert.

[Middle English *fesen*, to drive away, frighten, from Old English *fēsian*; akin to Swedish *fösa*, to drive, push.]

> ∾ *Phase* and *faze* get confused, mainly because many people do not know that there is such a word as *faze,* so they write *phase* instead. But this is a mistake.
>
> *Faze* is a verb and comes from Old English. It means to upset or bother someone. It is usually used in negative contexts, as in *She was not fazed by the setback but carried on as determined as ever.* By contrast, *phase* is both a noun and a verb, and it comes from Greek. The noun has the general meaning of "a stage of development," and it sees numerous uses in technical fields like chemistry and physics. The verb often occurs in the phrases *phase in* and *phase out,* which mean introducing or ending something one stage at a time.

A loud roar came from one of the side rooms, and startled me without fazing Sofia.

—John Grisham, *The Street Lawyer*

The enormous logistical and administrative complexities of running a big army fazed him not at all.

—Rick Atkinson, *The Day of Battle: The War in Sicily and Italy, 1943–1944*

29 **flounder** (floun′dər)

verb

1. To move clumsily or with little progress, as through water or mud. **2.** To act or function in a confused or directionless manner; struggle: *"Some [of the study's subjects] floundered professionally, never quite deciding what they wanted to do"* (Steve Olson, *Count Down*).

[Perhaps alteration of *founder* (probably influenced by words beginning with *fl-* and referring to halting or clumsy movement, such as *flop*).]

SEE NOTE AT **founder** (#30).

Jacinto said it would not be worthwhile to look for the mules. When the snow melted, he would recover the saddles and bridles. They **floundered** on foot some eight miles to a squatter's cabin, rented horses, and completed their journey by starlight.

—Willa Cather, *Death Comes for the Archbishop*

You can be truly smart and still struggle in life if you lack the ability to plan, organize time and space, initiate projects and see them through to completion, and you cannot resist immediate temptations in favor of later better rewards. When those capacities are damaged or underdeveloped, even people with intelligence and talent may **flounder**.

—Richard C. Saltus, "Lack Direction? Evaluate Your Brain's C.E.O.," *New York Times*, August 26, 2003

---

flounder / founder   **32**

30 founder (foun′dər)

verb

1. To sink below the surface of the water: *The ship struck a reef and foundered.* **2.** To cave in; sink: *The platform swayed and then foundered.* **3.** To fail utterly; collapse: *a marriage that soon foundered.*

[Middle English *foundren,* to sink to the ground, from Old French *fondrer,* from Vulgar Latin **funderāre,* from **fundus, *funder-,* bottom, from Latin *fundus, fund-.*]

≈ *Founder* and *flounder* are very similar words with similar meanings, but there is a subtle distinction in meaning that escapes many people.

The verb *founder* ultimately comes from the Latin word *fundus,* meaning "bottom" (also seen in *foundation*), and originally referred to knocking enemies down. In nautical use, it means "to sink to the bottom," as in *After striking the reef, the ship foundered.* The word has been extended figuratively to mean "to fail utterly; collapse": *The business had a promising start but foundered.* By contrast, *flounder* means "to move clumsily, thrash about," and hence, "to proceed in confusion." Thus, if a student is *foundering* in Chemistry 101, he had better drop the course; if he is *floundering,* he may yet pull through.

He had a strong dislike of making an arrest which was not followed by a charge of murder. If the case **foundered**, the accused was left under a pall of suspicion and the investigating officer could get a reputation for unwise and premature action.

—P. D. James, *The Private Patient*

31 free rein

noun

Unlimited freedom to act or make decisions.

> ❧ To grant someone *free rein* or (less commonly) *full rein* was originally a metaphorical extension of letting slack both reins on a horse, allowing the horse to go at its own pace and in the direction it found suitable. Since giving free rein or full rein is thus granting control and power to another, it is not surprising that these expressions have been understood as *free reign* or *full reign,* when the metaphor evokes the power that a monarch has over his or her dominion. But the expressions remain properly *free rein* or *full rein.*

A big yellow tiger-striped cat that apparently had **free rein** in the office walked across the desk top where Sallie was going on writing and rubbed against her arm, and made her frown.

—Richard Ford, "Puppy," *A Multitude of Sins*

He said, "Write about what you know. Take a dramatic incident with which you are familiar and go with it." I thought of my experience on the last flight to Czechoslovakia and gave my imagination **free rein.**

—Mary Higgins Clark, *All Through the Night*

A studious girl like Kate should certainly have been given **full rein** to take advantage of her courses at Barnard and spend some of her evenings scribbling, but the social side of life was not to be ignored, and she had to submit to a small dinner dance given her by one of Mama's well-endowed cousins and to attend a certain minimum of balls.

—Louis Auchincloss, "The Omelette and the Egg," *The Friend of Women and Other Stories*

32 **gambit** (găm′bĭt)

noun

1. An opening in chess in which the player risks one or more minor pieces, usually a pawn, in order to gain a favorable position. **2.** A maneuver, stratagem, or opening remark, especially one intended to bring about a desired result.

[Ultimately from Spanish *gambito,* an opening in chess in which the player risks a minor piece, from Italian *gambetto,* act of tripping someone up in wrestling, from *gamba,* leg, from Old Italian, from Late Latin, hoof, from Greek *kampē,* bend (as in a limb).]

SEE NOTE AT **gamut** (#33).

Washington now faced a vexing problem: the enlistments of his 3,400 Continental troops expired at midnight New Year's Eve; he decided to attack the Trenton Hessians while they slept off the effects of their Christmas celebration. After so many setbacks, it was a risky **gambit**; defeat could mean the end of the American cause. But a victory, even over a small outpost, might inspire lagging Patriots, cow Loyalists, encourage reenlistments and drive back the British—in short, keep the Revolution alive.

—Willard Sterne Randall,
"Hamilton Takes Command," *Smithsonian*

I've noticed that the opening **gambit** in conversation between two writers—and I'm always very uncomfortable hearing it—is "I like your work." I've heard it so often. It's so condescending. What if the person had not done any work? He would not be spoken to at all.

—Joseph Heller, *The Paris Review*

Every day flowers, chocolates, and the Mercedes-Benz came for Louise. She moved into a box at the theater, and supper afterward was alone with Bruno in an alcove at Schwamm's. He ran the entire **gamut** of breathless courtship, but best of all were the letters he wrote when he had to leave on a business trip abroad. Yes, it was these letters that won her.

—Ruth Prawer Jhabvala,
In Search of Love and Beauty

33 gamut (găm′ət)

noun

A complete range or extent: *a face that expressed the gamut of emotions, from rage to peaceful contentment.*

[Middle English *gamut*, musical scale, from Medieval Latin *gamma ut*, low G : *gamma,* lowest note of the medieval scale, denoted by the Greek letter gamma (from Greek *gamma,* gamma) + *ut,* first note of the lowest hexa-chord (after *ut,* first word in a Latin hymn to Saint John the Baptist, the initial syllables of successive lines of which were sung to the notes of an ascending scale CDEFGA (ut-re-mi-fa-sol-la) : Ut *queant laxis* / *Resonare fibris* / *Mira gestorum* / *famuli tuorum,* / Solve *polluti* / la*bii reatum* / *Sancte Iohannes,* "So that with the unrestrained fibers of their beings, your servants may make the won-ders of your deeds resound, remove the guilt from their unclean lip, Saint John!").]

๛ A *gamut* is the complete extent or range of something (in music, for example, where the word originated, it expresses the entire range of notes). Thus, to *run the gamut* is to tra-verse an entire range.

As is often the case with idioms, the original meanings of the words composing them can be lost, obscured, or con-fused. In this case, the uncommon word *gamut* is sometimes confused with the word *gambit.* Serious chess players know that a gambit is an opening move in which a minor piece like a pawn is risked or even sacrificed to gain a favorable posi-tion. Some people familiar with chess maintain that *gambit* should not be used in an extended sense except to refer to maneuvers that involve a tactical sacrifice or loss for some advantage. But *gambit* is well established in the general sense of "maneuver," and it does much service in the field of for-eign affairs and military strategy. *Gambit* is also used cor-rectly in the related sense of "a remark intended to open a conversation," in which there is no implication of risk, except for the risk of being rebuffed.

In any case, the phrase *run the gambit* is a mistake.

[New York Yankees manager Billy] Martin's tactics ran the gamut from training his players to run recklessly and in unexpected situations and ordering beanballs to intimidate opposing hitters, all the way to the clearly out-of-bounds areas of cultivating a staff of spitballers and stealing signs using stadium trickery.

— Derek Zumsteg, *The Cheater's Guide to Baseball*

---

34 **gibe** *also* **jibe** (jīb)

verb

To make taunting, heckling, or jeering remarks.

noun

A derisive remark.

[Possibly from Old French *giber*, to shake, use horseplay on, of unknown origin.]

> ∾ The words *gibe, gybe, jibe,* and *jive* sound alike (or nearly alike) and are easily confused. The word *gibe,* as a verb, means "to make taunting, heckling, or jeering remarks," as in *Quit gibing at me!* It may also be used as a noun meaning "a derisive remark." *Gibe* is sometimes spelled as *jibe,* and this inevitably leads to confusion with the verb *jibe* in the sense "to be in accord with or be consistent with" (as in *These figures don't jibe with what he led us to expect*). There is also a sailing term *jibe,* which means "to swing the sail from one tack to the other while running with the wind," and it is sometimes spelled *gybe.* Both variant spellings for these words are acceptable.
>
> The one outlier in this group, spelled with a *v,* is *jive,* which has origins in African American Vernacular English, and is first attested in 1928 as the title of a song by Louis Armstrong. As a noun, *jive* has several meanings: it refers to loose, misleading talk or conversation and was a kind of

---

dance associated with jazz in the 1930s. As a verb, it may mean "to mislead, kid, or taunt" or "to dance the jive."

Jive is occasionally used for *jibe* in American English, most commonly in sentences like *Her story doesn't jive with the facts,* but this usage is widely considered a mistake.

His catechism days were well behind him now, Matty's were, his days of blind belief, and he liked to **gibe** at his brother's self-conscious correctness, his attempts at analytical insight.

—Don DeLillo, *Underworld*

"We're talking the depths of the Cold War. We were fighting for our survival. We believed in what we were doing." I could not resist the **gibe**: "I imagine these days that comes a little harder."

—John le Carré, *Our Game*

CLOWN: This same skull, sir, was, sir, Yorick's skull, the King's jester.

. . . .

HAMLET: Alas, poor Yorick! I knew him, Horatio, a fellow of infinite jest, of most excellent fancy. . . . Where be your **gibes** now, your gambols, your songs, your flashes of merriment, that were wont to set the table on a roar?

—William Shakespeare,
Hamlet, Act 5, Scene 1, 180–191

35 gotten (gŏt′n)

verb

Past participle of *get*.

[Middle English *gote, goten,* past participle of *geten,* to get, from Old Norse *geta.*]

ᴄᴠ The notion that *gotten* is an illegitimate "nonword" has been around for over two hundred years and refuses to die. The word itself is much older than the criticism against it. As past participles of *get*, both *got* and *gotten* go back to the Middle Ages. In American English, *have got* is chiefly an intensive form of *have* in its senses of possession and obligation and can only be used in the present tense: *I have got three tickets to the game. We have got to improve our teamwork if we want to succeed. Gotten* sees regular use as a variant past participle of *get* and can occur in a variety of past and perfect tenses: *Had she gotten the car when you saw her? I would not have gotten sick if I had stayed home.* In Britain, *gotten* has mostly fallen out of use.

There are subtle distinctions in meaning between the two forms. *Got* often implies current possession, where *gotten* usually suggests the process of obtaining. Accordingly, *I haven't got any money* suggests that you are broke, while *I haven't gotten any money* suggests that you haven't been paid. This sense of process or progression applies to many other uses of *gotten,* and in some of these cases *got* just doesn't sound as natural to the American ear: *The bridge has gotten weaker since the storm. We have finally gotten used to the new software. Mice have gotten into the basement.*

Remember that only *got* can be used to express obligation, as in *I've got to go to Chicago.* The sentence *I have gotten to go to Chicago* implies that the person has had the opportunity or been given permission to go.

Also remember that in nonstandard usage, the *have* is often dropped from sentences using *got* or *gotten*, but that in standard usage the *have* is necessary (though it may be contracted as *'ve*). In standard English, *I've got to see that movie* expresses a desire as an obligation, whereas *I got to see that movie* means that you saw or were given permission to see the movie. In nonstandard English, *I got to* can express obligation or desire as well as make a statement about something that actually happened.

I had in mind quickly becoming a beloved genius. What I have **gotten** to be over almost a quarter of a century is a more or less respected writer. I know that I'm lucky to have **gotten** what I have. I'm acquainted with more gifted people who've worked harder on their writing than I have and haven't **gotten** anything.

—David Huddle, *The Writing Habit*

36 gybe (jīb)

verb and *noun*

Variant of **jibe¹**.

SEE NOTE AT **gibe** (#34).

37 historic (hĭ-stôr′ĭk)

adjective

1. Having importance in or influence on history. **2.** Historical.

[From Latin *historicus*, based on investigation of historical records, from Greek *historikos*, exact, precise, historical, from *historiā*, enquiry, historical account, from *historein*, to inquire, from *histōr*, learned man; akin to English *wise*.]

∾ *Historic* and *historical* have similar, though usually distinct, meanings. *Historic* refers to that which is associated with significant events in history: *the historic first voyage to the moon.* Thus, a historic house is likely to be of interest not just because it is relatively old, but because an important person lived in it or was otherwise associated with it. In contrast, *historical* refers more generally to that which happened in the past, regardless of significance: *a minor historical character in the novel, the historical architecture in the center of town.* These distinctions are not always observed, however, and a historic tour of a city might include the same sights as a historical tour. Therefore, it is important to make sure that the context indicates the intended meaning.

The early 1960s were thus a time of hope and a time of sorrow for black Americans, but above all a time of **historic,** unprecedented change.

—Tyler Stovall, *Paris Noir: African Americans in the City of Light*

38 **historical** (hĭ-stôr**′**ĭ-kəl)

adjective

1a. Of or relating to history; concerned with past events: *a historical account.* **b.** Based on or set in the past: *a historical novel.* **c.** Used in the past or providing evidence of the past: *historical weapons; historical records.* **2.** Important or famous in history. **3.** Concerned with phenomena as they change through time: *historical linguistics.*

[From Latin *historicus*, based on investigation of historical records (see **historic**, #37) + English *–al*, adjective suffix (from Middle English, from Old French, from Latin *–ālis*).]

SEE NOTE AT **historic** (#37).

His **historical** arguments that battle for its own sake was not necessarily the best approach earned him bitter enemies among that group of naval officers.

—Williamson Murray, "Corbett, Julian,"
The Reader's Companion to Military History,
edited by Robert Cowley and Geoffrey Parker

Not all virtues are equal to all people at all times. At certain **historical** moments some virtues may be more important than others.

—Mary Gordon, "Moral Fiction,"
The Atlantic Monthly, July 23, 2005

Most of those whose lives have been transformed by a **historical** crisis are impelled to return, at some point, to the site where the crisis occurred.

—Francine du Plessix Gray, "The Debacle,"
The American Scholar, Autumn 1999

39 **hoard** (hôrd)

noun

A hidden fund or supply stored for future use; a cache.

verb

1. To gather or accumulate a hoard. **2.** To keep hidden or private.

[Middle English *hord,* from Old English.]

ᘐ The words *hoard* and *horde* sound alike and can be confused. The word *hoard* is both a noun and a verb. A *hoard* is a cache, a hidden fund or supply stored for future use; to *hoard* something is to gather or accumulate a hoard of it, often obsessively. The word sometimes is used in the plural to mean "a great deal," as in *a financier with hoards of money.* *Hoard* is an old Germanic word derived from an Indo-European root.

The noun *horde,* which looks like a close cousin, is actually of Turkic origin and originally referred to a collection of families forming a tribe or group. In English, it is used to refer to any large group, especially a crowd or swarm. There is no verb *horde.*

Hoard is used primarily of inanimate objects and abstractions, while *horde* applies to people and other living things, such as insects. Only a horde of reporters should follow a movie star around, never a hoard. When large numbers of people are turning up in different places, the plural *hordes* is common: *hordes of students returning to campus, hordes of volunteers helping to get out the vote.*

He was a legend in Mississippi politics, the fixer, the inveterate meddler in local races, . . . the bank who could finance any race and funnel **hoards** of cash, the wise old man who led his party, and the thug who destroyed the others.

—John Grisham, *The Appeal*

She's more solicitous towards him than she's been in months—makes his favorite, milk jelly, for Sunday breakfast—though she knows that somehow this care is calculated, a **hoard** of love she's storing up in the hope she might draw on it later, if he finds out about the baby.

—Peter Ho Davies, *The Welsh Girl*

Under the blanket she **hoarded** the remains of the store bread.

—John Steinbeck, *The Grapes of Wrath*

Sanity is a valuable possession; I hoard it the way people once **hoarded** money. I save it, so I will have enough, when the time comes.

—Margaret Atwood, *The Handmaid's Tale*

 **horde** (hôrd)

noun

1. A large group or crowd; a swarm: *a horde of mosquitoes.* **2a.** A nomadic Mongol or Turkic tribe. **b.** A nomadic tribe or group.

[Ultimately (via words in Central and Eastern European languages such as German *Horde* and Polish *horda*) from Old Russian *orda,* from North-Western Turkic *ordï,* residence, court of a khan, from Old Turkic *ordu.*]

SEE NOTE AT **hoard** (#39).

The image of a **horde** of unthinking, cloned attackers is a classic science-fiction nightmare.

—Philip M. Boffey, "Fearing the Worst Should Anyone Produce a Cloned Baby," *New York Times,* January 5, 2003

A bell rings behind us, doors open with a whoosh, and **hordes** of screaming children run for the playground.

—Richard Lange, "Bank of America,"
Story Quarterly, 2002

Hordes of winged termites boiled out of their nests for their aerial nuptials.

—Ken Lamberton "The Wisdom of Toads,"
Puerto del Sol, Spring 1999

41 injustice (ĭn-jŭs′tĭs)

noun

1. Violation of another's rights or of what is right; lack of justice. **2.** A specific unjust act; a wrong.

[Middle English, from Old French, from Latin *iniūstitia,* from *iniūstus,* unjust : *in-,* not + *iūstus,* just; akin to Latin *iūs,* law, and *iūdex,* judge.]

∾ Usually the prefixes in the negatives of adjectives correspond to those in their noun forms, as in *indiscreet* and *indiscretion.* The word *just* is an exception to this pattern. The opposite of *just,* meaning "fair, equitable," is *unjust,* but the corresponding noun form of *unjust* is *injustice.* The forms *injust* and *unjustice* are usually not listed in dictionaries and are considered to be mistakes.

The Civil Rights Act is a challenge to all of us to go to work in our communities and our states, in our homes and in our hearts, to eliminate the last vestiges of **injustice** in our beloved country.

—President Lyndon B. Johnson, upon signing
the Civil Rights Act of 1964

I see no reason why good writers should not, if they have a bent that way, write angry protest novels about economic **injustice**.

—Doris May Lessing, *A Small Personal Voice*

All of us here know what it is to suffer for real need. That is a great **injustice**. But there is one injustice bitterer even than that—to be denied the right to work according to one's ability. To labor a lifetime uselessly. To be denied the chance to serve.

—Carson McCullers, *The Heart Is a Lonely Hunter*

42 **jibe**[1] *also* **gybe** (jīb)

verb

To shift a fore-and-aft sail from one side of a vessel to the other while sailing before the wind so as to sail on the opposite tack.

noun

The act of jibing.

[Alteration (perhaps influenced by *jib,* a triangular sail stretching from the foretopmast head) of *gybe,* from obsolete Dutch *gijben.*]

SEE NOTE AT **gibe** (#34).

All that day we sailed, from Newport Beach down the coast a few miles offshore, just outside the kelp beds, following the rhumb line, the shortest distance a navigator plots between two points, start to finish. No need to tack or **jibe**, just steer the compass heading of 145 degrees southeast, making small adjustments to the sails. Imi Loa was so fast that we left the hundreds of boats behind.

—William Booth, "Boat Camp," *Washington Post Magazine*

Then everything not secured came crashing down on everything else, the tables and chairs on the afterdeck went over, plates and bottles smashed, whatever was breakable immediately broke. The boat, the *Sans Regret,* fell off the wind like a comedian and flapped into a flying **jibe**.

—Robert Stone, *Bear and His Daughter*

jibe² (jīb)

verb

To be in accord; agree: *Your figures jibe with mine.*

[Origin unknown.]

SEE NOTE AT **gibe** (#34).

He started asking everyone who visited how he looked, and everyone said he looked great, so much better than a few weeks ago, which didn't **jibe** with what anyone had told him at that time.

—Susan Sontag, "The Way We Live Now,"
The New Yorker, November 24, 1986

Day after day, Sammy had listed to Anapol's lectures about taking the initiative, and the Science of Opportunity, and as these **jibed** with his own notions of how the world functioned, Sammy had believed.

—Michael Chabon, *The Amazing Adventures of Kavalier & Clay*

jibe³ (jīb)

noun and verb
Variant of **gibe**.

SEE NOTE AT **gibe** (#34).

Mostly he defended himself with biting sarcasm and sharp **jibes,** which left one slack-jawed and tongue-tied.

—Janna Malamud Smith, *My Father Is a Book:*
A Memoir of Bernard Malamud

He began to type up his notes on the Detroit factory. Again and again his mind drifted to Timmy, Timmy in his school on 19th Street now, being asked questions by the kids, being stared at, being **jibed** at because his father had been in prison.

—Patricia Highsmith, *The Glass Cell*

"I'd rather be dead or see you dead," I said, "than with another man. I'm not eccentric. That's ordinary human love. Ask anybody. They'd all say the same—if they loved at all." I **jibed** at her. "Anyone who loves is jealous."

—Graham Greene, *The End of the Affair*

 jive (jīv)

noun

1a. Jazz or swing music. **b.** The jargon of jazz musicians and enthusiasts. **2.** *Slang* Deceptive, nonsensical, or glib talk: *"the sexist, locker-room jive of men boasting and bonding"* (Trip Gabriel, *New York Times*).

verb

1. To play or dance to jive music. **2.** *Slang* To talk or speak to in an exaggerated, teasing, or misleading way.

adjective

Slang Misleading; phony or worthless.

[Origin unknown.]

SEE NOTE AT **gibe** (#34).

While Magic hobnobbed with Arkansas star Sidney Moncrief, blasting his boom box and **jiving** to the beat of the Ohio Players, Bird remained largely to himself, surveying the Kentucky scenery out the bus window while Magic's music—and personality—overtook the team.

> —Larry Bird and Earvin "Magic" Johnson,
> with Jackie MacMullan, *When the Game Was Ours*

A crowd of young black kids cruised by them, whistling and **jiving** at Charlie's outfit.

> —Jimmy Buffett, *Where Is Joe Merchant?*

"I said that your eyes are as limpid as a stream," I told her, remembering a line of nineteenth-century French Romantic poetry.

"Oh come on. You're **jiving** me. What's so beautiful about these brown eyes?" she teased me.

"What does '**jiving** me' mean?" I asked.

"It means that you are not telling the truth."

> —Manthia Diawara,
> *We Won't Budge: An African Exile in the World*

She really didn't like to talk to people too much anyway because all they ever wanted to talk about was **jive** nonsense.

> —Lolita Hernandez, "Autopsy of an Engine,"
> *Autopsy of an Engine and Other Stories from the Cadillac Plant*

lend (lĕnd)

verb

1a. To give or allow the use of something temporarily on the condition that the same or its equivalent will be returned. **b.** To provide money temporarily on the condition that the amount borrowed be returned, usually with an interest fee. **2.** To contribute or impart: *Books and a fireplace lent a feeling of warmth to the room.* **3.** To make available for another's use: *We lent our help after the storm.*

IDIOM:

lend (itself) to To accommodate or offer itself to; be suitable for.

[Middle English *lenden,* alteration of *lenen* (on the model of such verbs as *senden,* to send, whose past participle *sent* rhymed with *lent,* past participle of *lenen*), from Old English *lǣnan*; akin to Old Norse *lān,* loan.]

SEE NOTE AT **loan** (#48).

Mr. Matthew Adams, who had a pretty collection of books, and who frequented our printing-house, took notice of me, invited me to his library, and very kindly **lent** me such books as I chose to read.

—Benjamin Franklin, *The Autobiography of Benjamin Franklin*

Experience with death does not **lend** wisdom to physicians any more than to undertakers.

—Bernard Lown, *The Lost Art of Healing: Practicing Compassion in Medicine*

47 **load** (lōd)

noun

1a. Something that is carried, as by a vehicle, person, or animal: *a load of firewood.* **b.** The quantity that is or can be carried at one time. **2.** The amount of material that can be inserted into a device or machine at one time: *The washing machine has a full load.* **3a.** A mental weight or burden: *Good news took a load off my mind.* **b.** A responsibility regarded as oppressive.

[Middle English *lode,* alteration (influenced in meaning by *laden,* to load, from Old English *hladan*) of *lade,* course, way, from Old English *lād,* way; akin to Old English *lǣdan,* to lead.]

SEE NOTE AT **lode** (#49).

 48 **loan** (lōn)

noun

1. An instance of lending: *a bank that makes loans to small businesses.* **2a.** A sum of money that is lent, usually with an interest fee: *took out a loan to buy a car; repaid the loan over five years.* **b.** The agreement or contract specifying the terms and conditions of the repayment of such a sum. **3.** The state of being lent for temporary use: *a painting on loan from another museum.*

verb

To lend money or property.

[Middle English *lan, lon,* a loan, from Old Norse *lān;* akin to Old English *lǣnan,* to lend.]

∾ The verb *loan* has been criticized by usage writers since the 19th century as an illegitimate form. The verb had fallen out of use in Britain, and the British criticism of the word got picked up by writers in the United States, where the verb had survived. In fact, the use of *loan* as a verb goes back to the 16th century and possibly earlier. It has seen vigorous use in American English right up to today and must be considered standard.

Note that *loan* is used to describe only physical transactions, as of money or goods, while *lend* is correct not just for physical transactions, but for figurative ones as well.

In American English, *loan* is also (and primarily) used as a noun, but *lend* is never a noun. You go to the bank to get a loan, and the banker lends (or loans) you money. *Lend* is used as a noun outside of American English, specifically in northern England and Scotland, and in Australia and New Zealand.

"Let me tell you two gentlemen something about **loans**. A **loan** is not a gift. When we make a **loan**, we actually expect to get paid back."

—Tom Wolfe, *A Man in Full*

A new micro-credit scheme offers small **loans** to people with ideas for new businesses. So far, the repayment rate has been an impressive 98 percent.

—"Niger Delta: From Hijacking to Snail-Breeding," *The Economist*, March 12, 2002

They **loaned** him books to read and invited him to their house, and when they saw how smart he was, they told him that he should go to a university.

—Barack Obama, *Dreams from My Father*

49 lode (lōd)

noun

1a. The metal-bearing ore that fills a fissure in a rock formation. **b.** A vein of mineral ore deposited between clearly demarcated layers of rock. **2.** A rich source or supply.

[Middle English *lode,* way, load, from Old English *lād,* way; akin to *lǣdan,* to lead.]

> ∾ *Lode* and *load* are sometimes confused because they both refer to large quantities. The word *lode* means "a rich source or supply" and is usually used in reference to an ore deposit. A *mother lode* is the main vein of ore in a region. Metaphorically, it can be used for a particularly abundant source of something, as in a street that has the mother lode of ethnic restaurants in a city or a newsletter that claims to be a mother lode of investment ideas. The word *load* refers generally to a large amount of something and has a somewhat informal feel. Not surprisingly, *mother load* is a common misspelling.

In early planning for this project I felt a sense of returning to a new vein in the rich **lode** of Italian historical and musical source-materials in which I had previously worked on other topics.

—Lewis Lockwood, *Music in Renaissance Ferrara 1400–1505*

Oddly, though, finding love hadn't done much to improve Donna's mood; she was a worrier by nature, and the prospect of sharing her life with another person provided a **mother lode** of thorny new issues to fret about.

—Tom Perrotta, *The Abstinence Teacher*

noun

1. The greater number or part; a number more than half of the total. **2.** The amount by which the greater number of votes cast, as in an election, exceeds the total number of remaining votes. **3.** The political party, group, or faction having the most power by virtue of its larger representation or electoral strength.

[French *majorité*, from Medieval Latin *māiōritās*, from Latin *māior*, greater; akin to *magnus*, great.]

∾ The word *majority* refers to a number greater than 50 percent of the total of a group, also called an *absolute majority.* When there are more than two choices in question, as in many elections or surveys, the winner may receive more votes than any other in the group but less than 50 percent of the total. This is called a *plurality,* as in this newspaper article from the *Dallas Morning News:* "*Hispanic students in the Garland district have nearly overtaken white students' plurality, district records show.*" Sometimes, the word *majority* is used loosely to refer to the largest number in a group, but this can create ambiguity. For example, in the sentence *A majority of people surveyed didn't care where the new school was built so long as it was built within the next two years,* it is not entirely clear whether the group being referred to is a true majority or a plurality.

Both *majority* and *plurality* can also refer to the margin by which a contest has been won. Thus when a candidate wins an election by a majority of five votes, she wins five more votes than the votes for all of the other candidates combined. Similarly, when she wins by a plurality of five votes, she receives five more votes than that of the closest opponent.

51 masterful (măs′tər-fəl)

adjective

1. Acting or capable of acting as a master or leader, especially in being domineering or imperious. **2.** Having or showing mastery or skill; expert: *a masterful technique; masterful at filmmaking.*

[Middle English *maisterful* : *maister,* master (from Old English *māgister, mægister* and Old French *maistre,* both from Latin *magister*; akin to *magnus,* great) + *-ful,* full, from Old English *-full.*]

∾ It was H. W. Fowler who first recommended (back in 1926) that the word *masterful* be restricted to mean "imperious, domineering" (as in *a masterful tone of voice*), even though it had long been used to mean "having or showing the knowledge or skill of a master" as well. He wanted to restrict this latter meaning to the word *masterly,* as in *a masterly performance.* Many usage critics have since taken up his call.

But in practice, writers have been less heedful, and today *masterful* is well attested with the meaning "finely skilled." In fact, the word *masterful* is far more likely to occur before words like *performance* and *ability* than *masterly* is. This is not to say that *masterly* has gone by the board. It is still in frequent use by respected writers. The "domineering" sense of *masterful* is also in contemporary use, though with less frequency, and writers who use it tend to be traditionalists.

Pop stood short but **masterful** in the sweaters, and his belly sticking out, not soft but hard. He was a man of the hard-bellied type. Nobody intimidated Pop.
—Saul Bellow, "A Silver Dish," *The New Yorker*

Pretentious critics have expended an enormous amount of ink trying to portray Warhol as a **masterful** satirist, social commentator and visionary.
—Michiko Kakutani, "Andy Warhol," *New York Times Magazine,* November 17, 1996

Now let us rededicate ourselves to the long and bitter—but beautiful—struggle for a new world. This is the calling of the sons of God, and our brothers wait eagerly for our response. Shall we say the odds are too great? Shall we tell them the struggle is too hard? Will our message be that the forces of American life **militate** against their arrival as full men, and we send our deepest regrets?

—Martin Luther King, "A Time to Break Silence,"
April 4, 1967

52 masterly (măs′tər-lē)

adjective

Having or showing the knowledge or skill of a master.

[Middle English *maisterli* : *maister,* master (from Old English *māgister, mægister* and Old French *maistre,* both from Latin *magister*; akin to *magnus,* great) + *-li,* adjective suffix (from Old English *-līc*).]

SEE NOTE AT **masterful** (#51).

Together the two books present the strongest case for Koch as a **masterly** innovator, not merely a comedian of the spirit.

—David Lehman, "Dr. Fun,"
American Poetry Review, November 1995

Powell adjusted his aim and concluded with one of the more **masterly** *ad hominem* indictments in American newspaper history.

—David Rains Wallace, *The Bonehunters' Revenge: Dinosaurs, Greed, and the Greatest Scientific Feud of the Gilded Age*

53 militate (mĭl′ĭ-tāt′)

verb

To have force or influence; bring about an effect or a change.

[Latin *mīlitāre* (with past participle *mīlitātus*), to serve as a soldier, from *mīles, mīlit-,* soldier.]

SEE NOTE AT **mitigate** (#54).

There are aspects of workplace culture that **militate** in favor of making school a high priority. The most important of these is the role of managers in overseeing the educational performance of their younger charges.

—Katherine S. Newman, *No Shame in My Game: The Working Poor in the Inner City*

54 mitigate (mĭt′ĭ-gāt′)

verb

1. To moderate a quality or condition in force or intensity; alleviate. **2.** To take measures to moderate or alleviate something: *a program to mitigate against beach erosion.* **3.** To make alterations to land to make it less polluted or more hospitable to wildlife.

[Middle English *mitigaten,* from Latin *mītigāre* (with past participle *mītigātus*) : *mītis,* soft + *agere,* to drive, do.]

ᗡ The words *mitigate* and *militate* have entirely different meanings but are frequently confused. *Mitigate* means "to moderate the force or intensity of something; alleviate." Thus a judge might mitigate the sentence of a person convicted of a crime, technology can be designed to mitigate the effects of burning fossil fuels, and measures can be taken to mitigate the risks associated with overcrowding in school buildings.

Properly used, *militate* means "to have force or influence," and is often followed by a prepositional phrase starting with *in favor of, for,* or *against.* Thus, a judge might find that the evidence militates in favor of dismissing an indictment, the fact that a student population is especially large might militate for keeping older and younger students in separate wings of a building, and the proximity of a power plant to a neighborhood might militate against burning certain fuels.

Mitigate is sometimes followed by *against* when it means to take measures to alleviate something, as in *What steps can the town take to mitigate against damage from coastal storms?*

But using *mitigate* instead of *militate* is a mistake, as in this quote from the *New York Times:* "One Kerry strategist argued *that the stunningly high rates of early voting in some places could mitigate against sending the principals back, because it arguably reduces the additional gain from a candidate's visit."*

If events took a serious turn he would do what he could to **mitigate** the Emperor's displeasure, which he expected to be severe—and that was all that he could say at present.

—Robert Graves, *Claudius the God: And His Wife Messalina*

The watchman was snoring when he went out into the street. There he forced himself to take strides so long that the muscles of his legs rebelled, but the exercise failed to **mitigate** the chill he felt everywhere within him.

—Paul Bowles, *The Sheltering Sky*

Mr. Power, a much younger man, was employed in the Royal Irish Constabulary Office in Dublin Castle. The arc of his social rise intersected the arc of his friend's decline, but Mr. Kernan's decline was **mitigated** by the fact that certain of those friends who had known him at his highest point of success still esteemed him as a character.

—James Joyce, "A Mother," *Dubliners*

55 no holds barred

idiom

Without limits or restraints.

    ∾ The phrase *no holds barred* comes from wrestling, where a hold is "a manner of grasping or restraining an opponent." *No holds barred* refers to a match in which any kind of hold is legal. The phrase is often applied figuratively to other situations, where it indicates a lack of restraint or rules in the way something is done.

    The phrase is sometimes misunderstood as *no holes barred*. The metaphor is thus transformed to one in which holes in a container are left open (not obstructed or "barred") in order to let whatever is inside flow freely. The meaning of "lack of restraint" is still there, but the image is different. Remember to keep the *-d-*.

    Like many idioms, *no holds barred* is sometimes hyphenated and used as an adjective.

The two opposing groups charged at each other in a reckless, heedless assault, and there were **no holds barred**. There were fist fights and eye-gougings and ear-pullings. There were gang tackles, kicks to the groin, and hair-pullings. Four of them knocked me off Fox in the first furious charge. I found myself buried under a moving, grunting, angry pile of flesh.

—Pat Conroy, *The Lords of Discipline*

To see poverty in the police-state atmosphere of Latin America only provoked more strongly his desire to act, **no holds barred**, on behalf of peace and justice.

—Howard Zinn, *You Can't Be Neutral on a Moving Train: A Personal History of Our Times*

---

old (ōld)

adjective

1a. Having lived or existed for a relatively long time; far advanced in years or life. **b.** Relatively advanced in age: *Pamela is our oldest child.* **2.** Made long ago; in existence for many years: *an old book.* **3a.** Of or relating to a long life or to people who have had long lives: *a ripe old age.* **b.** Having or exhibiting the physical characteristics of age: *a prematurely old face.* **c.** Having or exhibiting the wisdom of age; mature: *a child who is old for his years.* **4.** Having lived or existed for a specified length of time: *She was 12 years old.* **5a.** Exhibiting the effects of time or long use; worn: *an old coat.* **b.** Known through long acquaintance; long familiar: *an old friend.* **c.** Skilled or able through long experience; practiced: *He is an old hand at doing home repairs.* **6a.** Belonging to a remote or former period in history; ancient: *old fossils.* **b.** Belonging to or being of an earlier time: *her old classmates.*

[Middle English *old,* from Old English *eald.*]

   ∾ *Old,* when applied to people, is a blunt term that usually suggests at least a degree of physical infirmity and age-related restrictions. It should be used cautiously, especially in referring to people advanced in years but leading active lives.

As a comparative form, *older* might logically seem to indicate greater age than *old,* but in most cases the opposite is true. A phrase such as *the older woman in the wool jacket* suggests a somewhat younger person than if *old* is substituted. Where *old* expresses an absolute, an arrival at old age, *older* takes a more relative view of aging as a continuum—older, but not yet old. As such, *older* is not just a euphemism for the blunter *old* but rather a more precise term for someone between middle and advanced age. And unlike *elderly, older* does not particularly suggest frailness or infirmity, making it the natural choice in many situations.

57 older (ōl′dər)

adjective

Comparative form of *old*.

[Middle English: *old* (from Old English *eald,* dialectal *ald*) + -*er,* comparative suffix (from Old English -*re,* -*ra*); Modern English *elder* represents the survival of the parallel Middle English form *elder,* from Old English *ealdra,* dialectal *eldra, yldra,* older, the comparative of *eald.*]

SEE NOTE AT **old** (#56).

58 ordinance (ôr′dn-əns)

noun

1. A statute or regulation, especially one that is enacted by a city government. **2.** An authoritative command or order. **3.** A custom or practice established by long usage. **4.** A Christian rite, especially the Eucharist.

[Middle English *ordinaunce,* from Old French *ordenance,* from Medieval Latin *ōrdinantia,* from Latin *ōrdināns, ōrdinant-,* present participle of *ōrdināre,* to ordain, from *ōrdō, ōrdin-,* order.]

 *Ordinance* and *ordnance* both derive from Latin *ōrdināre,* "to ordain," and are pronounced almost identically. They are thus easy to confuse. An *ordinance* is, most frequently, a statute or regulation, especially one enacted by a town, city, or county government. For instance, a town might have an ordinance against the public consumption of alcohol. *Ordinance* can also refer to an authoritative command or order or to a custom or practice established by long usage, such as a religious rite.

The term *ordnance* is less familiar to most people. It is a military term, referring either to military material, especially weapons, ammunition, and vehicles, or to the branch of an armed force that procures, maintains, and issues such equipment. Thus, the mission of the Ordnance Corps of the US Army is *"to support the development, production, acquisition and sustainment of weapons systems and munitions, and to provide Explosive Ordnance Disposal, during peace and war,* [in order] *to provide superior combat power to current and future forces of the United States Army."*

Ordnance is often used more restrictively to refer to munitions, including explosive weapons such as bombs, as in this quotation from Thomas Friedman writing in the *New York Times: "One arms cache alone found here* [in Fallujah, Iraq] *had 49,000 pieces of ordnance, ranging from mortars to ammo rounds."* Not surprisingly, *ordnance* is sometimes misspelled as *ordinance,* as in this quotation from ABC News online: *"The attackers were part-way through launching a cache of about nine home-made projectiles, however, when the remaining ordinance exploded in the vehicle."*

59 **ordnance** (ôrd′nəns)

noun

1. Military weapons, ammunition, combat vehicles, and equipment. **2.** The branch of an armed force that procures, maintains, and issues weapons, ammunition, and combat vehicles. **3.** Cannon; artillery.

[Middle English *ordnaunce*, variant of *ordinaunce*, order, military provision; see **ordinance** (#58).]

SEE NOTE AT **ordinance** (#58).

In the late 1850s . . . heavy rifled artillery . . . fired ogival rather than spherical projectiles. Capable of hitting accurately from ranges of several thousand yards, these quickly reduced masonry to rubble and forced another revolution in fortress architecture. The resultant fortresses of reinforced concrete, sunk low in the ground and defended by steel gun turrets, proved vulnerable in turn to heavy breech-loading **ordnance** firing high-explosive shells with time-delay fuses and sharply pointed noses of hard steel for penetration.

—John F. Guilmartin, "Siege Weapons," *The Reader's Companion to Military History,* edited by Robert Cowley and Geoffrey Parker

LeMay took his problems to statistical analysts. He wanted to jettison everything he did not need: he wanted to be able to fly below the bad weather and the jet stream; he wanted to break his bombers out of the usual rigid formation, which meant they could carry less fuel and more bomb tonnage. All of this, if he could do it, would allow him to load unprecedented **ordnance** onto his planes, almost all of it napalm or incendiaries. And it would allow him to fly low enough to drop the incendiaries in tight clusters, before wind could disperse their fires.

—James Carroll, *House of War*

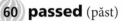

60 **passed** (păst)

verb

Past participle and past tense of *pass.*

[Middle English *passen*, from Old French *passer*, from Vulgar Latin *passāre*, from Latin *passus*, step; from past participle of *pandere*, to stretch, spread out.]

   ✤ *Passed* and *past* are easily confused. *Passed* is the past tense and past participle of the verb *pass: They passed several gas stations but forgot to fill up. The summer had passed slowly. Past* is the corresponding adjective (*in centuries past*), adverb (*The car drove past*), preposition (*We finally got past the crisis*), and noun (*living in the past*).

    Use of the correct form is not just a matter of spelling; the wrong sense can be conveyed by using the wrong word. For example, *The years passed in Canada were lonely* refers to a specific set of years spent by a particular person who was lonely during those years, while *The years past in Canada were lonely* refers to some unspecified set of years in the past, which were lonely in general.

61 **past** (păst)

adjective

1. No longer current; gone by; over: *His youth is past.* **2.** Having existed or occurred in an earlier time; bygone: *past events; in years past.* **3a.** Earlier than the present time; ago: *40 years past.* **b.** Just gone by or elapsed: *in the past few days.* **4.** Having served formerly in a given capacity, especially an official one: *a past president.* **5.** Of, relating to, or being a verb tense or form used to express an action or condition prior to the time it is expressed.

noun

1. The time before the present: *History is the study of the past.* **2a.** Previous background, career, experiences, and activities: *an elderly person with a distinguished past.* **b.** A former period of someone's life kept secret or thought to be shameful: *a family with a checkered past.* **3a.** The past tense. **b.** A verb form in the past tense.

adverb

So as to pass by or go beyond: *He waved as he walked past.*

preposition

1. Beyond in time; later than or after: *past midnight; a quarter past two.* **2.** Beyond in position; farther than: *The house is a mile past the first stoplight. They walked past the memorial in silence.* **3a.** Beyond the power, scope, extent, or influence of: *The problem is past the point of resolution.* **b.** Beyond in development or appropriateness: *The child is past drinking from a bottle. You're past sucking your thumb, so don't do it.* **4.** Beyond the number or amount of: *The child couldn't count past 20.*

[Middle English *past*, variant of *passed,* past participle of *passen*, to pass; see **passed** (#60).]

SEE NOTE AT **passed** (#60).

62 **peace** (pēs)

noun

1. The absence of war or other hostilities. **2.** An agreement or a treaty to end hostilities: *negotiated the peace.* **3.** Freedom from quarrels and disagreement; harmonious relations: *roommates living in peace with each other.* **4.** Public security and order: *a man who was arrested for disturbing the peace.* **5.** Inner contentment; serenity: *peace of mind.*

IDIOM:
keep *or* **hold (one's) peace** To be silent.

[Middle English *pes*, from Old French *pais, pes*, from Latin *pāx*.]

❧ The sound-alikes *peace* and *piece* are often confused when they appear in certain set expressions. Properly speaking, you have or seek *peace of mind*—a state of mental calm or tranquility. But peace of mind is not at all in play when you give someone *a piece of your mind*, that is, when you express your displeasure with or reprimand someone for something you are unhappy about. Originally, a piece of one's mind was just that—an opinion one had about something. But over the years the meaning of this expression has narrowed and become negative—you don't give someone a piece of your mind when you are offering congratulations or compliments or even condolences, only when you are expressing your dissatisfaction.

So writing *a peace of one's mind* is a mistake, although some writers have done so in jest or in trying to make a point (as when writing playfully about achieving mental tranquility). Be sure that the context makes clear that you are aware of the play on words if you use *peace* in this expression. Many people may not get the joke anyway.

By the same token, sentences like *She finally has piece of mind* will be viewed as mistakes by most readers.

Other expressions using these sound-alike nouns with verbs provide the occasion for further confusion and embarrassment. You might *say your piece* on a matter—say what you have to say about it, express your opinion. Here *piece* originally meant "a short written composition," and *saying your piece* meant reading it aloud (though no doubt the neutral use of *piece* meaning "opinion" has exerted some influence as well). In any case, you shouldn't *say your peace* about something unless you are deliberately playing with words, as in *Say your peace against violence!*

On the other hand, if you want to avoid saying what you think, you *keep* (or *hold*) *your peace*, that is, you preserve your peaceful outward state and remain silent when you might well have said something. The only time you should *keep* (or *hold*) *your piece* would be when *piece* means "a piece of something," like cake or pizza, or (if you are a gangster) "a gun."

"There is no **peace of mind** about health care for anyone in America unless you're a zillionaire."

—Dennis Rivera, quoted in "Dennis Rivera Leads Labor Charge for Health Reform," by Steven Greenhouse, *New York Times*

He had an instinct for knowing when to remain silent so as to gather everyone's attention and when to speak so that it would sound most impressive; thus, when he was expected to speak up, he often **held his peace** and stood against the furthest wall, and when he was expected to go silent and withdraw, he suddenly came forward and gave sharp utterance to his thoughts.

—Russell Banks, *Cloudsplitter*

63 **peremptory** (pə-rĕmp′tə-rē)

adjective

1a. Subject to no further debate or dispute; final and unassailable: *a peremptory decree*. **b.** Not allowing contradiction or refusal; imperative: *The officer issued peremptory commands*. **2.** Offensively self-assured; dictatorial: *a swaggering, peremptory manner*.

[Latin *peremptōrius*, from *peremptus*, past participle of *perimere*, to put an end to : *per-*, thoroughly + *emere*, to take, gain.]

SEE NOTE AT **preemptive** (#71).

Stuart was everywhere that morning, seeing and being seen, leading troops forward and rallying them when they fell back. His battle tactics were not subtle. He had taken Jackson's corps where he found it at midnight, and under Lee's **peremptory** orders he felt obliged to attack at dawn, without waiting to rearrange his forces or to explore the enemy line for a weak spot.

—Stephen W. Sears, *Chancellorsville*

Polly had brought from home the habit of starting off her sentences with the name of the person she was specifically addressing. "Lorna—" she would say, or "Brendan—" Lorna had forgotten about this way of talking. It seemed to her now rather **peremptory** and rude. Most of Polly's sentences at the dinner table began with "Lorna—" and were about people known only to her and Polly.

—Alice Munro, "Post and Beam," *The New Yorker,*
December 11, 2000

noun

1. A distinct stage of development: *"The American occupation of Japan fell into three successive phases"* (Edwin O. Reischauer). **2.** A temporary manner, attitude, or pattern of behavior: *His sullenness is just a passing phase.* **3.** An aspect; a part: *We must reconsider every phase of the operation.* **4.** *Astronomy* **a.** One of the cyclically recurring apparent shapes of the visibly illuminated portion of the moon or a planet. **b.** The relative configuration, measured in angular units such as degrees or radians, of two orbiting bodies that periodically eclipse. **5.** *Physics* **a.** A particular stage in a periodic process or phenomenon. **b.** The fraction of a complete cycle elapsed as measured from a specified reference point and often expressed as an angle. **6.** *Chemistry* **a.** Any of the forms or states, solid, liquid, gas, or plasma, in which matter can exist, depending on temperature and pressure. **b.** A discrete homogeneous part of a material system that is mechanically separable from the rest, as is ice from water. **7.** *Biology* A characteristic form, appearance, or stage of development that occurs in a cycle or that distinguishes some individuals of a group: *the white color phase of a weasel; the swarming phase of locusts.*

verb

phase in To introduce, one stage at a time.

phase out To bring or come to an end, one stage at a time.

[French *phase,* phase of the moon, stage, from Latin *phasis,* from Greek *phasis,* appearance, from *phainein,* to show.]

SEE NOTE AT **faze** (#28).

The first **phase** of the cleanup, which ran from May to October of last year, turned up more contamination than expected in some areas.

—Mireya Navarro, "Adjustments Likely in Hudson
River Cleanup," *New York Times,* January 22, 2010

In the mid-1990s, an attempt by the Clinton administration to enact a miniscule four-cent-a-gallon energy tax, in hopes of gradually **phasing in** a carbon-reduction regime, caused a revolt in Congress so severe that Clinton essentially shelved the idea.

—Paul Roberts, *The End of Oil: On the Edge
of a Perilous New World*

65 **piece** (pēs)

noun

1. A thing considered as a unit or an element of a larger thing, quantity, or class; a portion: *a piece of string.* **2.** A portion or part that has been separated from a whole: *a piece of pie.* **3.** An object that is one member of a group or class: *a piece of furniture.* **4.** An artistic, musical, or literary work or composition: *"They are lively and well-plotted pieces, both in prose"* (Tucker Brooke). **5.** An instance; a specimen: *a piece of sheer folly.* **6.** A declaration of one's opinions or findings: *speak one's piece.* **7.** A coin: *a ten-cent piece.* **8a.** One of the counters or figures used in playing various board games. **b.** Any one of the chess figures other than a pawn. **9.** *Slang* A firearm, especially a rifle. **10.** *Informal* A given distance: *"There was farm country down the road on the right a piece"* (James Agee).

a piece of (one's) mind Frank and severe criticism; censure.

say (one's) piece To express one's opinion; say what one thinks.

[Middle English *pece,* from Old French, from Vulgar Latin **pettia,* probably of Celtic origin.]

SEE NOTE AT **peace** (#62).

I wanted to cry most of all because I had wanted to right my own wrongs, to raise a loving family, and I had instead produced a hellion. A hellion! She would pursue us through our lives, fueled by rage, crashing into the nursing home where I would sit slumped over in a wheelchair, to give me **a piece of her mind.**

—Jane Hamilton, *A Map of the World*

Russell encouraged us to consider whether the pacific Bartleby, by preferring to do nothing, was making a gesture in protest of his situation or was simply not much good with his hands and therefore destined to be acted upon by a world that kept the hard knocks coming in a steady stream. At least that's what I took him to mean, and I got busy parlaying it into a general discussion in which Russell, having **said his piece,** declined to participate further.

—Carlo Rotella, "Cut Time," *Cut Time: An Education at the Fights*

66 plurality (plŏŏ-răl′ĭ-tē)

noun

1. A large number or amount; a multitude. **2a.** In a contest of more than two choices, the number of votes cast for the winning choice if this number is not more than one half of the total votes cast. **b.** The number by which the vote of the winning choice in such a contest exceeds that of the closest opponent.

[Middle English *pluralite,* from Old French, from Late Latin *plūrālitās,* from Latin *plūrālis,* plural, from *plūs, plūr-,* more.]

SEE NOTE AT **majority** (#50).

Mrs. Squeers, when excited, was accustomed to use strong language, and, moreover, to make use of a **plurality** of epithets, some of which were of a figurative kind.

—Charles Dickens, *Nicholas Nickleby*

On November 6, 1860, Abraham Lincoln won the American presidency in a unique election that foreshadowed the division of the nation. Four candidates, including two Democrats, had contested what became a referendum on sectional allegiances. . . . With a numerical power that threatened the South, Northerners supported Lincoln. And so Lincoln won, with a substantial majority of electoral votes, a **plurality** of 40 percent of the popular vote, and 54 percent of the North's votes. He had received less than 3 percent of the South's ballots. The Illinoisan was the first member of the recently organized Republican party to win the presidency, and he would be the only president-elect in American history whose victory, even before his Inauguration, would significantly affect national events.

—Jean H. Baker, "Abraham Lincoln," *The Reader's Companion to the American Presidency,* edited by Alan Brinkley and Davis Dyer

 **67 pore** (pôr)

verb

To read, study, or examine carefully and attentively.

[Middle English *pouren*, of unknown origin.]

∞ Although the verbs *pore* and *pour* are pronounced identically, as (pôr), by many people, these two words should be distinguished in spelling. Unaware that the verb *pore* exists, many writers use *pour* instead. *Pore* means "to read or study something intently." It is mainly used in the phrase *pore over.*

Naturally, the idea of *pouring* a liquid over something so as to cover it is easily evoked by the sound of the words *pore over,* and people may interpret the verb as a metaphor— pouring one's vision over a document.

Whatever the reasons for the confusion, *pore* and *pour* should be kept distinct since they have different meanings and etymologies. Note that the object of *pore* can be things other than written texts, such as photographs.

At the local library, I **pored** over documents and microfilm I requisitioned from the Library of Congress.

—Laura Hillenbrand, "A Sudden Illness," *The New Yorker,*
July 7, 2003

When, at her insistence, we showed her our photo albums embossed with the designs of butterflies, she **pored** over the snapshots that chronicled the ceremony.

—Jhumpa Lahiri, "The Treatment of Bibi Haldar,"
The Interpreter of Maladies

Another thing about Jamie is, she can cook. Not hot-dogs and hamburgers like me, but real, honest-to-good gourmet stuff. When my grandparents came to stay with us the first week in February, Jamie did all the cooking. Every night, before they went to sleep, Grandma and Jamie **pored** over cookbooks deciding on the menu for the following day.

—Judy Blume, *Forever*

68 **pour** (pôr)

verb

1a. To cause a liquid or granular solid to stream or flow, as from a container: *She poured tea from the pot into the cup.* **b.** To pour a liquid or particles into a container: *I poured a glass of milk.* **c.** To empty a container of a liquid or granular solid: *The girl poured a bucket of sand on the ground.* **2a.** To stream or flow continuously or profusely: *Water poured over the dam.* **b.** To rain hard or heavily: *It has been pouring for an hour.* **3a.** To send forth, produce, express, or utter copiously, as if in a stream or flood: *The company poured money into the project; poured out my inner thoughts.* **b.** To pass or proceed in large numbers or quantity: *Students poured into the auditorium.*

[Middle English *pouren*, perhaps from Old North French *purer*, to pour out, squeeze (fruit), winnow, from Latin *pūrāre*, to purify, from *pūrus*, pure.]

SEE NOTE AT **pore** (#67).

69 **practicable** (prăk′tĭ-kə-bəl)

adjective

1. Capable of being effected, done, or put into practice; feasible. **2.** Usable for a specified purpose: *a practicable way of entry.*

[Medieval Latin *prācticābilis*, capable of being used, from *prācticāre*, to practice, from *prāctica*, practice, from Greek *prāktikē*, practical science, from feminine of *prāktikos*, fit for action, practical, from *prāssein*, *prāk-*, to make, do.]

It is easy to confuse *practical* and *practicable* since they look so much alike and overlap in meaning. *Practicable* has only two meanings: "feasible" (as in *Sharon came up with a practicable plan*) and "usable for a specified purpose" (as in *A new, more practicable entrance was added to the house*). Note that *practicable* cannot be applied to persons.

Practical has six meanings, all related. These range from "acquired through practice rather than theory" (*I have practical experience using a lathe*) to "sensible" (*He has always been a practical guy*) to "virtual" (*The banquet was a practical fiasco*). It also has the sense "capable of being put into effect, useful," wherein the confusion with *practicable* arises. But a distinction between these words remains nonetheless: For the purpose of ordering coffee in a Parisian café, it would be *practical,* that is, useful, to learn some French, but it still might not be *practicable* for someone with a busy schedule and little time to learn.

The passage of the vehicles might have been **practicable** if empty; but built up with hay to the bedroom windows as one was, it was impossible.

—Thomas Hardy, *The Mayor of Casterbridge*

St. Francis's ideal of poverty was **practicable** then, because it held up for admiration a way of life not so enormously unlike the actual way of his humbler contemporaries.

—Aldous Huxley, *Point Counter Point*

The only **practicable** means of impressing one's pecuniary ability on these unsympathetic observers of one's everyday life is an unremitting demonstration of ability to pay.

—Thorstein Veblen, *The Theory of the Leisure Class*

70 practical (prăk′tĭ-kəl)

adjective

1. Of, relating to, governed by, or acquired through practice or action, rather than theory, speculation, or ideals: *He gained practical experience sailing as a deck hand.* **2.** Manifested in or involving practice: *practical applications of calculus.* **3.** Capable of or suitable to being used or put into effect; useful: *She has practical knowledge of Japanese.* **4.** Concerned with the production or operation of something useful: *Woodworking is a practical art.* **5.** Having or showing good judgment; sensible: *We need to be practical about how we approach this problem.* **6.** Being actually so in almost every respect; virtual: *The party was a practical disaster.*

[Middle English *practicale,* from Medieval Latin *prācticālis,* from *prāctica,* practice; see **practicable** (#69).]

SEE NOTE AT **practicable** (#69).

"I'm a **practical** man," Mr. Pearn began. "This is a **practical** world. I've had much **practical** experience. So I ask what will Greek and Latin do to help me in **practical** affairs? The answer is nothing. We people here, we don't have the time for frills. We have to learn **practical** things. Education should be **practical**, teaching trades and **practical** science."

—James T. Farrell, *My Days of Anger*

71 **preemptive** (prē-ĕmp'tĭv)

adjective

Undertaken or initiated to deter or prevent an anticipated, usually unpleasant situation or occurrence: *The two companies organized a preemptive alliance against a possible takeover by another firm.*

[English *pre-*, before, pre- (from Middle English, from Old French, from Latin *prae-*, from *prae*, before, in front) + Latin *ēmptus*, past participle of Latin *emere*, to take, gain + English *-ive*, adjective suffix (from Middle English, from Old French, from Latin *–īvus*).]

∾ The original meaning of *preemptive* was "having the quality or the power of preemption," where *preemption* was a previously established right to purchase something before others do: *The preemptive purchase of the land by the settlers resulted in very few newcomers to the area.* Its sense has extended to describe any activity that is undertaken before an adversary can act, and the word is used today especially to describe military engagements designed to destroy enemy forces before they can attack, as in *a preemptive air strike.*

Perhaps due to the latter usage, along with a similarity in sound and spelling, *preemptive* is sometimes confused with *peremptory*. *Peremptory* has a range of meanings, including "putting an end to all debate or action" (*The court issued a peremptory decree*); "not allowing contradiction or refusal; imperative" (*The lawyers for each side are entitled to some peremptory challenges dismissing potential jurors*); "having the nature of or expressing a command; urgent" (*The teacher spoke in a peremptory tone*); and "offensively self-assured; dictatorial" (*a swaggering, peremptory manner*). Since a preemptive military action can be thought of as peremptory, the two words are sometimes confused. They should be kept distinct.

To sum up: a preemptive action is one that is undertaken to prevent an adversary from acting first; a peremptory action is one undertaken from arbitrary power or a belief in an unquestionable right.

The ability to achieve a decisive strategic surprise in the opening stage of a war magnifies volatility in times of crisis; this reciprocal fear of surprise attack in turn creates strong incentives for making the first move or launching a **preemptive** attack.

—Michael I. Handel, "Surprise," *The Reader's Companion to Military History*, edited by Robert Cowley and Geoffrey Parker

Older people . . . tend to cut back their social networks selectively, preserving positive relationships. That strategy makes good biological sense. As we grow old, our health inevitably becomes more fragile; as cells age and die, our immune system and other bulwarks for good health work less and less well. Dropping unrewarding social ties may be a **preemptive** move to manage our own emotional states for the better.

—Daniel Goleman, *Social Intelligence: The New Science of Human Relationships*

72 rationale (răsh′ə-năl′)

noun

The fundamental reasons for something; the basis for something.

[From Late Latin *ratiōnāle*, from neuter of Latin *ratiōnālis*, rational, from *ratiō*, *ratiōn-*, reason, from *ratus*, past participle of *rērī*, to consider, think.]

∾ The word *rationale* is a noun, referring to the fundamental reasons or the basis for something: *The rationale behind the college's introductory writing course is that every student should be able to write well-constructed essays as soon as possible.* The word *rationalization* is also a noun, but it is derived from the verb *rationalize*, which means "to make rational, to interpret rationally," and "to devise self-serving reasons to justify something." Each sense of the verb thus describes a mental process, and *rationalization* commonly refers to the result of one of these processes: *Their rationalization of farm production was unsuccessful.* This meaning is not strictly synonymous with *rationale*, especially since *rationalization* commonly suggests a post-hoc, self-serving process. *A rationale for their behavior* is an actual rational basis for their actions, while *a rationalization of their behavior* suggests an attempt to defend unreasonable actions.

India's independence in 1947 had destroyed the strategic rationale for Britain's presence in the Middle East.

—Anthony Cave Brown, *Oil, God, and Gold:*
The Story of Aramco and the Saudi Kings

73 rationalization (răsh′ə-nă-lĭ-zā′shən)

noun

The act, process, or practice of explaining or interpreting something rationally or of devising self-serving reasons to justify something.

[From *rationalize,* from *rational,* from Middle English *racional,* from Old French *racionel,* from *ratiōnālis,* rational; see **rationale** (#72).]

SEE NOTE AT **rationale** (#72).

Not learning Setswana was something Ray held against himself. His original rationalization, because that was what it was, for not learning any particular African language had been that there was no telling where in the continent he might be posted next.

—Norman Rush, *Mortals*

This is a trick most perpetrators use, especially those sponsored by a powerful government, to try to make their actions understandable by saying, "What my people have done, yours have done too." What is tragic is that they

really do believe that what they have done is no worse than the other group's actions. Typically, the perpetrator starts off with **rationalization,** to convince himself of the legitimacy of his acts, then he begins to communicate his **rationalization** to others. At this point it is no longer a **rationalization** but a "truth" that releases the perpetrator from any sense of guilt he may still feel about his evil deeds. If the enemy is doing the same thing he himself is engaged in, then he can't be that bad.

—Gobodo Madikeizela, *A Human Being Died That Night: A South African Woman Confronts the Legacy of Apartheid*

 74 relegate (rĕl′ĭ-gāt′)

verb

1. To place in an inferior or obscure place, rank, category, or condition: *an artist's work that is now relegated to storerooms; a group that has been relegated to the status of second-class citizens.* **2.** To refer or assign a matter or task, for example, for decision or action: *The college relegated the teaching of writing to graduate students. The Senate relegated the matter to a committee.*

[Middle English *relegaten,* to banish, from Latin *relēgāre, relēgāt-* : *re-,* back, backwards, again + *lēgāre,* to send, depute (from earlier "to commission by contract," from *lēx, lēg-,* law).]

∾ Both *relegate* and *delegate* involve assigning someone or something to a particular role or condition, and this similarity, along with their similar sound, leads to occasional confusion. *Relegate* has a physical sense, in which it means "to assign someone or something to a position, especially an obscure or inferior position." It often seems a synonym of *put aside* or *banish,* as in *relegated to the dustbin of history* or *relegated to the back of the bus.*

Relegate also refers to categorization, where it refers to the classifying of something in a particular manner. Often the category in question is an inferior one: *Pluto has been relegated to the category of dwarf planet.*

In addition, *relegate* means to assign something, such as a responsibility, to someone for a decision or action, and here is where the word comes close to being a synonym of *delegate*: *The contract dispute was relegated to arbitration.*

Delegate does not have a physical sense, although the word often entails human movement. *Delegate* refers to the entrusting of a task or responsibility to another, as in *He avoids delegating work to his employees.* It can also mean "to authorize a person to act as one's representative," as in *The executive director and those delegated to act on her behalf have the responsibility for upholding confidentiality.*

Relegate thus commonly has the negative connotation of dismissal or even condemnation, while *delegate* is a more neutral or somewhat positive term, suggesting commitment and responsibility.

Rice, the NFL's career leader in touchdowns, receptions and yards receiving, was a non-factor during much of the game and at times was **relegated** to the sidelines.
—Dennis Georgatos, "Rice Refutes Selfish Portrayal," *Augusta Chronicle*, November 24, 1998

Within a few years, these human beings will be **relegated** to an abstract category called "the underclass."
—James McPherson, "Ivy Day in the Empty Room," *Iowa Review*, 1993

Nixon fought the impeachment, arguing that the Senate should not be allowed to **relegate** the matter to a committee.
—Anne E. Kornblut, "Rehnquist Has Strict View on Impeachment," *Boston Globe*, January 3, 1999

 **repress** (rĭ-prĕs′)

verb

1. To put down by force, usually before total control has been lost; quell: *The government repressed the rebellion.* **2.** To hold back by an act of volition: *He couldn't repress a smirk.* **3.** To exclude (painful or disturbing memories, for example) automatically or unconsciously from the conscious mind. **4.** To block transcription of a gene by combination of a protein to an operator gene.

[Middle English *repressen*, from Latin *reprimere, repress-* : *re-*, back, backwards (also used as an intensive prefix) + *premere*, to press.]

෨ The verbs *repress* and *suppress* have similar meanings, but there are subtle differences that are worth paying attention to. Both share the general sense of holding back or subduing something, but *repress* suggests keeping something under control to maintain or regulate order, while *suppress* suggests a more active curtailment, even an active fight against an opposing force. Thus, *The government repressed the rebellion* implies that the government always maintained control and that the rebellious forces never posed a serious threat to governmental power before being put down, while *The government suppressed the rebellion* suggests that a significant rebellion was under way and that the government had to react strongly to put an end to it. Similarly, you repress (rather than suppress) a smirk in order to maintain a serious appearance (with the implication that you are in control of your demeanor), and one would take a medicine that suppresses (rather than represses) a cough in order to reduce its severity (because the cough has proven to be beyond your ability to control).

Both words also see use in psychology, and here a similar distinction prevails. *Repress* generally means "to exclude painful or disturbing memories automatically or unconsciously from the conscious mind." *Suppress* means "to exclude unacceptable desires or thoughts deliberately from the mind." Using *repress* to express a conscious effort, as in *For years he tried to repress his frightful memories,* would technically be incorrect. A repressed memory is one that someone has placed beyond recall not by deliberate effort but as part of the mind's unconscious attempt to protect itself.

The British monarch's method of choice for **repressing** his colonial subjects was the accusation of sedition. When the King wanted to crush colonial opposition, he looked to the law of seditious libel.

—Susan Dunn, *Jefferson's Second Revolution: The Election Crisis of 1800 and the Triumph of Republicanism*

Michael, hardly daring to stir lest he be seen, buried his face in his sleeve against the trunk to **repress** the laughter welling up in him.

—Robert Stone, *Bay of Souls*

The story is presented not as a distressing or painful experience that was **repressed** but as one of the many little disappointments that happen and are simply forgotten.

—Elaine Tuttle Hansen, *Mother Without Child: Contemporary Fiction and the Crisis of Motherhood*

76 **restive** (rĕs′tĭv)

adjective

1a. Uneasily impatient under restriction, opposition, criticism, or delay: *Passengers on board the delayed airliner began to grow restive.* **b.** Showing a pressing desire for change; unsettled or dissatisfied: *a restive feeling.* **2.** Refusing to move. Used of a horse or other animal.

[From Middle English *restif*, stationary, refusing to go forward (as for example a stubborn horse), unruly, from Old French, from *rester*, to remain, from Latin *restāre*, to stay back, linger, remain : *re-*, back, backwards + *stāre*, to stand.]

∞ The adjectives *restive* and *restless* overlap in meaning but have subtle distinctions. *Restive* usually indicates impatience or uneasiness caused by external coercion or restriction. *Restive* also has a related sense, "stubbornly resisting control," and is sometimes applied to horses to mean "balky."

Restless can mean "characterized by a lack of rest," as in *a restless night*. It can also mean "constantly moving or acting," as in *restless seas* or *A plot hatched in his restless brain*. The confusion with *restive* arises when *restless* means "characterized by unrest, fidgety" and "dissatisfied with one's current situation." But unlike *restive, restless* is usually not used in contexts involving external force or restriction.

In some cases, both restraint and restlessness are implied so that the words can be used interchangeably, as in the following quotation from the *Florida Times-Union:* "*Federal courtrooms are stodgy places except on those increasingly rare days of naturalization ceremonies. It was a noisy place Wednesday as mothers tried to quiet restive children with juice boxes and Fritos.*"

This afternoon she was peculiarly **restive**. She would really like to do something of which her well-wishers disapproved.

—E. M. Forster, *A Room With a View*

It was hard to take the measure of a man who displayed the flaccid composure of a corpse. No brow is noble when it is dead: it has no need to be. This lad seemed about as close to death as one could be and still harbor hope of recovery, yet the sense she had about him was neither tranquil nor **restive**.

—Gregory Maguire, *Wicked: The Life and Times of the Wicked Witch of the West*

It was fully realised that though the human beings had been defeated in the Battle of the Cowshed they might make another and more determined attempt to recapture the farm and reinstate Mr. Jones. They had all the more reason for doing so because the news of their defeat had spread across the countryside and made the animals on the neighbouring farms more **restive** than ever.

—George Orwell, *Animal Farm*

restless (rĕst′lĭs)

adjective

1. Characterized by a lack of quiet, repose, or rest: *I spent a restless night sleeping on the floor.* **2a.** Not able to rest, relax, or be still: *a restless child.* **b.** Never still or motionless: *the restless sea.* **3.** Having or showing a pressing desire for change or action: *She started to feel restless in her job.*

[Middle English *resteless,* finding no rest or respose, from Old English *restlēas* : *rest,* rest + *-lēas,* -less (from *lēas,* without, free from).]

SEE NOTE AT **restive** (#76).

He was bidden by his confessor to name some sin of his past life before absolution was given him. He named it with humility and shame and repented of it once more. It humiliated and shamed him to think that he would never be freed from it wholly, however holily he might live or whatever virtues or perfections he might attain. A **restless** feeling of guilt would always be present with him: he would confess and repent and be absolved, confess and repent and be absolved again, fruitlessly.

—James Joyce, *A Portrait of the Artist as a Young Man*

His fat delicate hands rested on the glass, the fingers moving like small **restless** sausages.

—John Steinbeck, *Cannery Row*

The man whose future empire would be intertwined with the twentieth-century multinational corporation began by studying the records of the conquistadors. The research whetted his appetite and made him **restless**.

—Adam Hochschild, *King Leopold's Ghost*

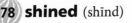 **shined** (shīnd)

verb

Past tense and past participle of *shine.*

[From Middle English *shinede,* past tense of *shinen,* to shine, from Old English *scīnan* (with past tense *scān,* ancestor of Modern English *shone*).]

    ∿ The verb *shine* has two different past tenses, *shined* and *shone,* and these forms also function as past participles. The past tense and past participle *shone* is more frequently used when the verb means "to emit light, be luminous": *The full moon shone brilliantly in the east.* The form *shined,* on the other hand, is frequently used when the verb means "to direct a beam of light" or "to polish," as in *He shined his flashlight down the dark staircase* or *The butler shined the silver.* Nevertheless, each form is sometimes used, and used acceptably, where the other might be expected. When meaning "to polish," however, *shined* is the only form that sounds correct: *He had never had his shoes shined* [not *shone*] *by a real shoe-shiner before.* As a policy, writers are best advised to reserve *shone* for the meaning "to emit light" and to use *shined* elsewhere.

He **shined** his own shoes daily in the morning before opening the store we lived over.

—Donna Caruso, *Journey Without a Map: Growing Up Italian: A Memoir*

Celeste stopped and **shined** her light into the trees. Quickly something moved outside the hoop of brightness. Another crash and crunch. Was something or someone shadowing her there in the woods?

—Sara Pritchard, *Lately*

79 **shone** (shōn)

verb

Past tense and past participle of *shine*.

[From Middle English *shone*, past tense of *shinen*, to shine, from Old English *scān*, past tense of *scīnan*, to shine.]

SEE NOTE AT **shined** (#78).

Stiff and cold, she lay on her stomach. When she arched her neck, she could see the black sky and sharp sickle moon that **shone** starkly through a break in the leaves.

—Mary Sharratt, *The Real Minerva*

He wore purple-and-black running shoes with shards of neon-green reflectors on the heels. It was the reflectors that reminded me I'd seen him earlier—it had surprised me how they **shone** even on this gray, wet day.

—Angela Patrinos, "Sculpture 1,"
The New Yorker, July 24, 1995

80 **sleight of hand** (slīt′ əv hănd′)

noun

1a. The performance of or skill in performing juggling or magic tricks so quickly and deftly that the manner of execution cannot be observed; legerdemain. **b.** A trick or set of tricks performed in this way. **2a.** Deception or trickery. **b.** A deceptive or misleading act.

    The word *sleight of hand* is often miswritten as *slight of hand* because of the identity of sound in the words *sleight*, meaning "a trick performed so deftly that the manner of execution cannot be observed," and *slight*, meaning as an adjective "small, delicate, of little importance" and as a noun "a snub, a discourteous inattention." The mistake may also result from a notion associating dexterity with lightness of weight and thus slightness of size—an idea also suggested by the synonym *legerdemain,* a borrowing of the French phrase meaning "light of hand." In the past, *slight* was actually a common spelling for the word "sleight," but now the two words are consistently kept apart in standardized spelling.

Despite this history and the sameness of sound, *sleight* and *slight* are different words in origin. *Sleight* comes from Middle English *sleghthe,* "slyness, cunning," which is a borrowing of Old Norse *slœgdh. Slœgdh* is in turn the noun corresponding to the Old Norse adjective *slœgr,* "sly." *Slœgr* too was borrowed into Middle English, in fact, and spelled *sleigh*—the ancestor of the Modern English adjective *sly.* In this way, Modern English *sleight* is simply the noun corresponding to the adjective *sly. Slight,* on the other hand, belongs to a group of words occurring in the Germanic languages (the close relatives of English) originally meaning "level, plain, simple," then by extension "without note, worthless, bad," such as the German word *schlecht,* "bad."

A magician of professional grade, he once dazzled me with **sleights of hand** I could not fathom even when he repeated them a foot or two from my concentrated gaze.

—E. O. Wilson, *Naturalist*

Jefferson thought that all the paper money issued by banks was nothing but a swindle, some sort of **sleight of hand**, and not to be compared with the "solid wealth" produced by "hard labor in the earth."

—Gordon S. Wood, *Revolutionary Characters: What Made the Founders Different*

81 slew¹ (slo͞o)

noun

Informal A large amount or number; a lot: *a slew of unpaid bills.*

[Irish Gaelic *slua*, multitude, from Old Irish *slúag*.]

❧ The noun *slew*, pronounced (slo͞o), means "a large amount or number; a lot," as in *a slew of unpaid bills.* The word is fairly colloquial and should be replaced by expressions such as "a great number" in more formal writing. The word comes from Irish Gaelic *slua*, "army, multitude."

There is also a verb spelled *slew*, which is not to be confused with the *slew* that is the past tense of the verb *slay.* This *slew* means "to turn sharply, veer": *She braked and slewed the car around. The car slewed around and headed back toward us.* This verb has a variant spelling, *slue*, which appears to be the older form of the word. The origin of the word *slew/slue* is unknown, but it is probably unrelated to the other words that are pronounced (slo͞o).

Another *slew* is a variant spelling of the word that is usually spelled *slough.* This word has several meanings and pronunciations. One of these is "a swamp, especially one with trees, that forms part of a bayou, inlet, or backwater." In the United States, the pronunciation (slo͞o), rhyming with *brew*, is usual in this meaning, but the pronunciation (slou), rhyming with *brow*, can be heard as well. *Slough* also has the related meaning "a hollow filled with deep mud." Frequently, *slough* is used metaphorically to indicate a state of deep despair or a place characterized by immorality, in reference to the *Slough of Despond*, where sinners become mired in the allegorical novel *Pilgrim's Progress* by John Bunyan. In this extended usage, and in the phrase *Slough of Despond*, the pronunciation (slou) is perhaps more usual. In British English, (slou) is also the usual pronunciation of the word in all senses related to the meaning "muddy terrain." The word comes from Old English *slōh.*

Measures of land and geographic features are often used to specify quantities, as in expressions like *a mountain of work* and *a sea of troubles.* This tendency, as well as the homophony between *slew* and *slough* in the United States, has resulted in the misspelling of the *slew* that means "a lot" as *slough.* This mistake frequently occurs when masses or quantities of unpleasant or tedious things are being measured, as in *I had to deal with a whole slough* [properly *slew*] *of problems* or *I could offer you a whole slough* [properly *slew*] *of reasons.*

To complicate matters further, there is a different word spelled *slough.* It means "a layer or mass of dead tissue," and it is used in particular of the dead outer skin shed by a reptile or amphibian. The word also has a related verbal sense, "to be cast off or shed," as in *The snake sloughed off its skin.* In these meanings, *slough* is pronounced (slŭf), rhyming with *tough.* The spelling of this word as *sluff* is usually considered an error, even in the slang meaning of the phrasal verb *slough off,* "to be lazy, shirk," as in *He's been sluffing off at work.* The word *slough* in the sense of "to cast off" is unrelated to *slough,* "swamp," and first appeared in Middle English as *slughe.*

Don't get the idea, Stan, that because during the war salesmen were hard to hire, now, when there's a lot of men out of work, there aren't a **slew** of bright young fellows that would be glad to step in and enjoy your opportunities.

—Sinclair Lewis, *Babbitt*

In his second term, the president [Richard Nixon] proceeded to shred even more of [economist Milton] Friedman's orthodoxies, passing a **slew** of new laws imposing higher environmental and safety standards on industry.

—Naomi Klein, *The Shock Doctrine: The Rise of Disaster Capitalism*

He had a **slew** of orange crates all filled with beautiful scholarly books, some of them in Oriental languages, all the great sutras, comments on sutras, the complete works of D. T. Suzuki and a fine quadruple-volume edition of Japanese haikus.

—Jack Kerouac, *The Dharma Bums*

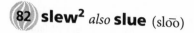 **slew²** *also* **slue** (slo͞o)

verb

1. To turn or cause to turn on an axis; rotate or spin.
2. To turn or slide, or cause to turn or slide sharply; veer or skid.

[Origin unknown.]

The three of them made it to where the snowmobile had **slewed** around and stalled out. Hallorann sat the woman down on the passenger seat and put her coat on. He lifted her feet up—they were very cold but not frozen yet—and rubbed them briskly with Danny's jacket before putting on her boots. Wendy's face was alabaster pale, her eyes half-lidded and dazed, but she had begun to shiver. Hallorann thought this was a good sign.

—Stephen King, *The Shining*

"Tell me what you know about Mark Callender."
The violet eyes **slewed** from door to window as if desperate for escape.
　"I wasn't there when he did it."
　"When who did what?"

—P. D. James, *An Unsuitable Job for a Woman*

But as soon as he had turned and before he had taken a step forward into the valley he heard a noise behind him. It was only a small noise but it sounded loud in that immense silence. It froze him dead-still where he stood for a second. Then he **slewed** round his neck and looked.
　At the bottom of the cliff a little on his left was a low, dark hole—the entrance to a cave perhaps. And out of this two thin wisps of smoke were coming.

—C. S. Lewis, *The Voyage of the Dawn Treader*

 **83 slew³** (slōō)

noun
Variant of **slough¹**.

SEE NOTE AT **slew¹** (#81).

84 slough¹ *also* **slew** (slōō, slou)

noun
1. A depression or hollow, usually filled with deep mud or mire. **2.** *also* **slue** A stagnant swamp, marsh, bog, or pond, especially as part of a bayou, inlet, or backwater. **3.** A state of deep despair or moral degradation.

[Middle English, from Old English *slōh*.]

SEE NOTE AT **slew¹** (#81).

As the blue columns took to the roads on January 20, the skies opened, and soldiers, horses, and wagons soon found themselves in a vast **slough**.
—Edwin C. Fishel, *The Secret War for the Union: The Untold Story of Military Intelligence in the Civil War*

She could feel his attention straining toward her, fully expecting her, . . . the family friend who had once danced with him in her arms, to lift him with some glib wisdom out of the dreary **slough** of his present predicament.
—Gail Godwin, *A Southern Family*

If you feel destiny calling, and see, as I see, a future of endless possibility stretching before us; if you sense, as I sense, that the time is now to shake off our slumber, and **slough** off our fear, and make good on the debt we owe past and future generations, then I'm ready to take up the cause, and march with you, and work with you.

—Barack Obama, upon
announcing his candidacy for
President of the United States,
February 10, 2007

85 slough² (slŭf)

noun

1. The dead outer skin shed by a reptile or amphibian. **2.** A layer or mass of dead tissue separated from surrounding living tissue, as in a wound, sore, or inflammation. **3.** An outer layer or covering that is shed.

verb

1. To be cast off or shed; come off: *The snake's skin sloughs off.* **2.** To shed a slough: *The snake sloughed its skin.* **3.** To discard as undesirable or unfavorable; get rid of: *After he got the new job he sloughed off his former associates.* **4.** To separate from surrounding living tissue. Used of dead tissue.

[Middle English *slough, slogh,* akin to Middle High German *slūch, sluoch,* snakeskin (Modern German *Schlauch,* hose, tire tube).]

SEE NOTE AT **slew¹** (#81).

 **slue** (slo͞o)

verb

Variant of **slew²**.

SEE NOTE AT **slew¹** (#81).

He was backing up an incline that had seemed level on the way in but showed itself as a remorselessly long hill, studded with rocks and deep in snow. His incoming tracks twisted like rope. He forced out another twenty feet, spinning the tires until they smoked, and then the rear wheels **slued** sideways off the track and into a two-foot ditch, the engine died, and that was it.

—Annie Proulx, "The Half-Skinned Steer,"
The Atlantic, November 1997

 **suppress** (sə-prĕs′)

verb

1. To put an end to forcibly; subdue: *The government suppressed the rebellion.* **2.** To curtail or prohibit the activities of: *The government tends to suppress dissident groups.* **3.** To keep from being revealed, published, or circulated: *The opposing lawyer suppressed evidence. The censors tried to suppress the film.* **4.** To deliberately exclude unacceptable desires or thoughts from the mind. **5.** To inhibit the expression of: *She had to suppress her anger during the interview.* **6.** To restrain the growth, activity, or release of: *The doctors did everything they could to suppress the virus.*

[Middle English *suppressen*, from Latin *supprimere, suppress-* : *sub-*, under, beneath + *premere*, to press.]

SEE NOTE AT **repress** (#75).

Even a totalitarian regime that ruthlessly **suppressed** political opposition by terror operated on the premise that it was desirable to retain mass political support among the German people.

—Daniel B. Silver, *Refuge in Hell:
How Berlin's Jewish Hospital Outlasted the Nazis*

By such methods it was found possible to bring about an enormous diminution of vocabulary. . . . All that was necessary, in any case where two words formed a natural pair of opposites, was to decide which of them to **suppress**. *Dark*, for example, could be replaced by *unlight*, or *light* by *undark*, according to preference.

—George Orwell, "Newspeak," Appendix to *1984*

After exposure to distressing films, people who are instructed to **suppress** thoughts related to the film later experience more film-related intrusive memories than those who do not try to **suppress**. Attempts to avoid thinking about a horrendous experience are common in trauma survivors, but are more likely to amplify, rather than lessen, later problems with persisting memories.

—Daniel L. Schacter, *The Seven Sins of Memory*

 88 tenant (tĕn′ənt)

noun

A person who pays rent to use or occupy land, a building, or other property owned by another.

[Middle English *tenant*, from Old French, from present participle of *tenir*, to hold, from Latin *tenēre*.]

SEE NOTE AT **tenet** (#89).

Mr. Biswas, as a driver, was given an end room. The back window had been nailed shut by the previous **tenant** and plastered over with newspaper. Its position could only be guessed at, since newspaper covered the walls from top to bottom.

—V. S. Naipaul, *A House for Mr. Biswas*

She had no job anymore, no permanent address, and when she failed to return to her room at the Fitzwilliam Arms in downtown Los Angeles for the rest of that week in early 1929, the desk clerk had her belongings carried down to the basement and rented her room to someone else. There was nothing unusual about that. People disappeared all the time, and you couldn't leave a room empty when a new **tenant** was willing to pay for it.

—Paul Auster, *The Book of Illusions*

89 **tenet** (tĕn′ĭt)

noun

A doctrine, principle, or position held as part of a philosophy, religion, or field of endeavor.

[From Latin *tenet*, (he, she, or it) holds, third person singular present indicative of *tenēre*, to hold (used in early modern philosophical writings in Latin to introduce the opinion held by a person).]

∾ *Tenet* is sometimes misspelled as *tenant* or *tenent*. This may be because the word *tenant* is so abundantly familiar, while *tenet* is not, or because there are many words that end in –*ent* and are used in contexts where beliefs are being discussed, that is, where the word *tenet* is likely to show up. Among these –*ent* words are *argument*, *cogent*, and *tangent*.

Another factor leading to the confusion may be the nasal sounds in *tenet* and *tenant/tenent*. The *n* in the word *tenet* may have made the following vowel *e* slightly nasal, leading people unfamiliar with the word *tenet* to perceive it as being the same as the word *tenant*. People may also see *tenet* as being formed from a word element *ten–* (as in *tenacious*) and the common suffix *–ent*, the way *tangent* is built from *tang–* (found in *tangible*) and *nutrient* is built from *nutri–* (found in *nutrition*).

Also encouraging the misspelling of *tenet* as *tenant* is the tendency of *tenant* to be pronounced with the second *n* skipped over or weakly spoken (as "tennit," so to speak), in much the same way that the word *varmint* gets pronounced as *varmit*.

Whatever the explanation, the misspelling of *tenet* as *tenant* or *tenent* is a frequent error that you should avoid: *The tenets* [not *tenents*] *of Christianity appealed to the common people of the Roman Empire.*

"That's what my therapist calls them—you know, the things we all have that ground us, and not just people but tenants and—"

"**Tenets**?" I asked.

"Huh?"

"**Tenets**," I said. "Tenants are people who live in your building. **Tenets** are principles, articles of faith."

"Right. That's what I said. **Tenets** and principles and, you know, the little sayings and ideals and philosophies we hold on to to get us through the day."

—Dennis Lehane, *Prayers for Rain*

Physicists working in Europe announced yesterday that they had passed through nature's looking glass and had created atoms made of antimatter, or antiatoms, opening up the possibility of experiments in a realm once reserved for science fiction writers. Such experiments, theorists say, could test some of the basic **tenets** of modern physics and light the way to a deeper understanding of nature.

—Dennis Overbye, "More Sci- than Fi-: Physicists Create Antimatter," *New York Times*, September 19, 2002

throe (thrō)

noun

1. A severe pang or spasm of pain, as in childbirth.

2. *often* **throes** A condition of extreme difficulty, struggle, or trouble.

[Middle English *throwe, thrawe,* probably partly from Old English *thrāwu, thrēa,* punishment, affliction, pang, and partly from Old English *thrōwian,* to suffer, and partly from Old Norse *thrā,* throe, struggle, obstinacy.]

∾ The noun *throe* is an odd-looking word and it is sometimes confused with the familiar noun and verb *throw,* which sounds just like it. This confusion is understandable because in its literal use *throe* refers to a spasm attended by pain, and so it can suggest violent movement, the way one might thrash around or throw one's body about in pain.

Throe usually occurs in the phrase *in the throes of,* where it can indicate a physical ordeal such as childbirth or death, but it can also be used figuratively of any kind of ordeal or situation of difficulty, even for an institution or for society at large.

Ka-Boom! The elephant's knees buckled at the shot. He pitched forward, driving his tusks into the ground and balancing on them for a moment. Then he hauled himself upright, and charged. The poachers fired again, but the elephant seemed determined to kill before he died. He quickly gained on one of the fleeing poachers, but just as he was about to crush the man, he stopped. His massive body convulsed, and he rolled onto his side, shivering in his death **throes.** In seconds the poachers began hacking at his tusks with their machetes.

—Mark and Delia Owens, *Secrets of the Savanna:*
Twenty-three Years in the African Wilderness
Unraveling the Mysteries of Elephants and People

Here the honest but inflexible servant clapped the door to and bolted it within.

This was the climax. A pang of exquisite suffering—a **throe** of true despair—rent and heaved my heart. Worn out, indeed, I was; not another step could I stir. I sank on the wet doorstep: I groaned—I wrung my hands—I wept in utter anguish.

—Charlotte Brontë, *Jane Eyre*

By the time he returned for the Second Continental Congress, in late spring 1775 . . . Philadelphia had become the capital of a revolution. . . . Congress was in the **throes** of creating an army, appointing a commander-in-chief, issuing the first Continental money.

—David McCullough, *John Adams*

91 toe the line *or* toe the mark

idiom

To adhere to doctrines or rules conscientiously; conform or do as one is told.

↬ The idioms *toe the line* and *toe the mark* mean "to adhere to doctrines or rules conscientiously; conform." The phrases go back to the 19th century and according to the *Oxford English Dictionary* probably started in the British navy. There were similar phrases that have not survived, like *toe the scratch* and *toe the crack*. All of these phrases conjure a scene in which people step up to a line shoulder to shoulder as in military formation or at the start of a race, in preparation for action of some kind.

The idiom *toe the line* is often misspelled as *tow the line,* as in this Salt Lake City newspaper: "*Most of us have forgotten those filmstrip projectors, usually set up on a student's desk in preparation for a story with a message: how to feel safe, how to tow the line with authorities, how to get excited about the moon and outer space."* The mistake is easy to make because the image of towing a line and pulling a load fits neatly with the requirements of conformity and submission.

By the approach of evening at the end of the first full day on Parris Island, the recruits' identities have been hollowed out. They know very little about anything, except **toeing the line**, which they are getting good at doing. The entire platoon can now be on line in just three seconds, down from twenty last night, and five this morning.

—Thomas E. Ricks, *Making the Corps*

Owens went to the starting line for his heat. . . . He looked at the four white men and the Asian who were also **toeing the line**. Then he put his head down and waited for the gun.

—Jeremy Schaap, *Triumph: The Untold Story of Jesse Owens and Hitler's Olympics*

"But at a time like this there's no room for—well—personal views. The man who doesn't **toe the line** is lost."

—E. M. Forster, *A Passage to India*

I hear all over that he's simply just *pleading* with her to marry him, but I don't know how true that is. I'm sure I can't see why he'd want to, but then you never can tell what a man like that will do. It would be just good enough *for* him if he got her, that's what I say. Then he'd see. She'd never stand for any of his nonsense. She'd make him **toe the mark**. She's a smart woman.

—Dorothy Parker, "Lady with a Lamp," *Harper's Bazaar*, April 1932

92 **unexceptionable** (ŭn'ĭk-sĕp'shə-nə-bəl)

adjective

Beyond any reasonable objection; irreproachable.

[*un-* (from Middle English, from Old English) + *exceptionable* : *exception* (from Middle English *excepcioun,* from Old French *exception,* from Latin *exceptiō, exceptiōn-,* from *exceptus,* past participle of *excipere,* to exclude : *ex-,* out + *capere,* to take) + *-able* (from Middle English, from Old French, from Latin *-ābilis, -ibilis*).]

> ∾ The adjectives *unexceptionable* and *unexceptional* are sometimes confused. *Unexceptionable* is derived from the word *exception* in its sense "objection," as in the idiom *take exception.* Thus *unexceptionable* means "not open to any objection." *Unexceptional,* in contrast, generally means "not exceptional, not varying from the usual."

The largest refreshment booth in the fair was provided by an innkeeper from a neighbouring town. This was considered an **unexceptionable** place for obtaining the necessary food and rest: Host Trencher (as he was jauntily called by the local newspaper) being a substantial man of high repute for catering through all the country round.

—Thomas Hardy, *Far from the Madding Crowd*

Some twenty years ago, long before Dolly showed it was plausible, a book was published claiming, in great detail, that a rich man in South America had had himself cloned, by a scientist code-named Darwin. As a work of science fiction it would have been **unexceptionable**, but it was sold as sober fact.

—Richard Dawkins, *A Devil's Chaplain*

93 unexceptional (ŭn′ĭk-sĕp′shə-nəl)

adjective

Not varying from a norm; usual.

[*un-* (from Middle English, from Old English) + *exceptional* : *exception* (from Middle English *excepcioun*, from Old French *exception*, from Latin *exceptiō*, *exceptiōn-* , from *exceptus*, past participle of *excipere*, to exclude : *ex-*, out + *capere*, to take) + *-al*, adjective suffix (from Middle English, from Old French, from Latin *−ālis*).]

SEE NOTE AT **unexceptionable** (#92).

I saw my neighbour gardening, chatted with him for a time, and then strolled in to breakfast. It was a most **unexceptional** morning.

—H. G. Wells, *The War of the Worlds*

This paltry tale seems as **unexceptional** as a trip to the supermarket.

—Jack Todd, *Desertion: In the Time of Vietnam*

His physical appearance must have been **unexceptional**, since few of those who knew him firsthand can recall anything about how he looked, other than the fact that he was small, "only a little man."

—Daniel B. Silver, *Refuge in Hell: How Berlin's Jewish Hospital Outlasted the Nazis*

adjective

1. Violating principles of justice or fairness; unfair: *an unjust law.* **2.** Acting in violation of such principles: *an unjust ruler.*

[Middle English *unjuste* : *un-*, un- (from Old English) + *juste*, just (from Old French, from Latin *iūstus*; akin to Latin *iūs*, law, and *iūdex*, judge).]

SEE NOTE AT **injustice** (#41).

How does one determine when a law is just or **unjust**? A just law is a man-made code that squares with the moral law, or the law of God. An **unjust** law is a code that is out of harmony with the moral law. To put it in the terms of Saint Thomas Aquinas, an **unjust** law is a human law that is not rooted in eternal and natural law. Any law that uplifts human personality is just. Any law that degrades human personality is **unjust**. All segregation statutes are **unjust** because segregation distorts the soul and damages the personality.

—Martin Luther King, Jr., "Letter from Birmingham Jail," April 16, 1963

95 venal (vē′nəl)

adjective

Given to or characterized by corrupt dealings, especially bribery: *a venal police officer.*

[Latin *vēnālis*, from *vēnum*, sale.]

> The words *venal* and *venial* look and sound similar but have very different meanings. In general, *venal* refers to monetary corruption. A venal police officer is one who is given or susceptible to bribery or is otherwise capable of betraying scruples for a price. The word derives from Latin *vēnum*, "sale." *Venial*, from the Latin *venia*, "forgiveness," means "easily excused or forgiven," as in *a venial offense. Venial* is most often found in the phrase *venial sin*, which is sometimes extended to nonreligious contexts. In Catholic theology, a venial sin is one that is minor and that does not incur damnation. It stands in contrast to *mortal sin.*

The people with the technical skills to organise a war economy, the experience to draw up multi-million-livre contracts and run them successfully . . . were either **venal** by habit, because the business of government finance in previous decades had been run as a **venal** enterprise, or they had acquired venality through their weakness when confronted by great sums.

—David Andress, *The Terror: The Merciless War for Freedom in Revolutionary France*

Villa was soon able to add another couple of corrupt gringos to his payroll. In Washington he retained the services of the **venal** lobbyist Sherbourne G. Hopkins, who would work for anyone as long as the pay was good enough, and was not above working for opposing sides simultaneously and selling each one's secrets to the other.

—Frank McLynn, *Villa and Zapata: A History of the Mexican Revolution*

96 **venial** (vē′nē-əl, vēn′yəl)

adjective

1. Easily excused or forgiven; pardonable: *a venial offense.* **2.** *Roman Catholic Church* Minor, therefore warranting only temporal punishment: *a venial sin.*

[Middle English, from Old French, from Late Latin *veniālis*, from Latin *venia*, forgiveness.]

SEE NOTE AT **venal** (#95).

I am not so indifferent, Mrs. Bounderby, as to be regardless of this vice in your brother, or inclined to consider it a **venial** offence.

—Charles Dickens, *Hard Times*

Sometimes he had amused himself by putting difficult questions to me, asking me what one should do in certain circumstances or whether such and such sins were mortal or **venial** or only imperfections.

—James Joyce, "The Sisters," *Dubliners*

97 **waive** (wāv)

verb

1. To give up or relinquish a claim or right voluntarily. **2.** To refrain from insisting on or enforcing (a rule or penalty, for example); dispense with: *"The original ban on private trading had long since been waived"* (William L. Schurz). **3.** To refrain from engaging in an activity, sometimes temporarily; cancel or postpone: *Let's waive our discussion of that problem.*

[Middle English *weiven*, to abandon, from Anglo-Norman *weyver*, from *waif*, ownerless property, stray animal;

---

venial / waive

probably from a Scandinavian source akin to Old Norse *veif*, anything that flaps or waves; and to Latin *vibrāre*, to vibrate, both from the Indo-European root *weip-, *weib-, to turn, vacillate, vibrate.]

☙ *Wave*, meaning "to move freely back and forth or up and down in the air," is sometimes confused with *waive*, especially when it is followed by a preposition such as *off* or *aside* to mean "dismiss" or "disregard," as in this example from the *Scotsman*: "*For if senior civil servants and the Executive can waive aside due legal process and parliamentary accountability so readily, why should voters believe or act differently?*"

Sometimes *wave* is miscast for *waive* in its general meaning of "relinquish." Interestingly, it is easy to imagine *wave aside* making sense in the following example from the *Calgary Sun*, where *wave* by itself is erroneous: "*Zeta-Jones says it's a tradition for performers to sing their nominated songs, and she's not about to break with that tradition even if rapper Eminem has waved the same honour.*"

As they entered the house he earnestly entreated her to name the day that was to make him the happiest of men; and though such a solicitation must be **waived** for the present, the lady felt no inclination to trifle with his happiness.

—Jane Austen, *Pride and Prejudice*

The attorneys contended that their clients had been unjustly convicted because legal counsel had not been appointed them until after they had confessed and had **waived** preliminary hearings; and because they were not competently represented at their trial, [and] were convicted with the help of evidence seized without a search warrant.

—Truman Capote, *In Cold Blood*

wangle (wăng′gəl)

verb

1. To obtain or achieve something by cleverness or deceit, especially in persuading someone: *She wangled the job even though she had no training.* **2.** To extricate oneself by subtle or indirect means, as from difficulty: *He wangled out of a shift at work by pretending to be sick.*

[Perhaps expressive alteration of earlier *waggle,* to wag back and forth quickly, wield, manipulate, from *wag,* from Middle English *waggen;* akin to Middle English *wiglen,* to wiggle, probably from Middle Low German *wiggelen,* to totter.]

SEE NOTE AT **wrangle** (#100).

He lived at the dump in a neat tarpaper lean-to with a sign reading "Dump Custodian" on the skew-hung door. He had **wangled** a space heater out of that skinflint board of selectmen three years ago, and had given up his apartment in town for good.

—Stephen King, *Salem's Lot*

I had sent Lonoff a packet of my first published short stories, along with an earnest introductory letter, and in this way managed to **wangle** the dinner invitation that had turned into an overnight stay only because bad weather had prevented me from departing till the next day.

—Philip Roth, *Exit Ghost*

99 wave (wāv)

verb

1. To move freely back and forth or up and down in the air, as branches in the wind. **2.** To cause to move back and forth or up and down, either once or repeatedly: *She waved a fan before her face.* **3a.** To make a signal with an up-and-down or back-and-forth movement of the hand or an object held in the hand: *We waved as she drove by.* **b.** To move or swing as in giving a signal: *He waved his hand.* **c.** To signal or express by waving the hand or an object held in the hand: *We waved goodbye.* **d.** To signal a person to move in a specified direction: *The police officer waved the motorist into the right lane.* **4.** To arrange into curves, curls, or undulations: *wave one's hair.*

[Middle English *waven*, from Old English *wafian*, to move the hand up and down, wave; akin to Old English *wefan*, to weave cloth, and Old Norse *vefa*, to weave cloth, from the Proto-Indo-European root **webh-*, to weave cloth.]

SEE NOTE AT **waive** (#97).

Languidly, at the edge of the underwater flooring, something that looked vaguely like a human arm and hand in a dark sleeve **waved** out from under the submerged boarding.

—Raymond Chandler, *Trouble Is My Business*

A great cheer went up from the crowd packed onto the sidewalk for four blocks to the bleachers. Flags flew over the heads of the crowd, a boulevard of flags, and small children hoisted onto their parents' shoulders **waved** tiny flags—a solid wall of humanity with little faces poking out between the legs.

—Garrison Keillor, *Liberty: A Novel of Lake Wobegon*

One of the boys came out of the water, shining like a new car. He **waved** to me. Andy LeBlanc from my school, a year ahead of me. I **waved** back, thinking there was no way he would have known who I was. Then I thought that maybe he was **waving** just because I was a girl in a swimsuit, sitting on the bank of the river. He probably didn't even know we went to school together. For some reason that made it even better.

—Ann Patchett, *The Patron Saint of Liars*

He dragged ashore the cook, and then waded toward the captain; but the captain **waved** him away and sent him to the correspondent.

—Stephen Crane, *The Red Badge of Courage*

100 **wrangle** (răng**′**gəl)

verb

1a. To quarrel noisily or angrily. **b.** To win or obtain something by argument: *I wrangled a free ticket to a show.* **2a.** To grasp and maneuver something. **b.** To attempt to deal with or understand something; contend or struggle: *"In the lab . . . students wrangle with the nature of discovery" (New York Times).* **3.** To herd horses or other livestock. **4.** To grasp and maneuver something; wrestle.

[Middle English *wranglen,* of Middle Low German origin; akin to Old English *wringan,* to twist, wring.]

   ∽ The verbs *wrangle* and *wangle* sound similar and are sometimes confused. *Wrangle* usually means "to quarrel noisily or angrily," as well as "to herd horses or other livestock." Thus people wrangle with one another or with the IRS or some other agency.

   Wangle generally means "to achieve by contrivance or manipulation," as in *He wangled a job for which he had no training* and *The reporter wangled a copy of the preliminary report from one of the committee members.* Properly speaking, one does not wangle with someone else.

   On the other hand, most dictionaries accept that one may also wrangle something for oneself (that is, win something by argumentation), so in this sense the two words are synonyms. Thus, it is Standard English to wangle or wrangle an invitation to a party, but the latter involves putting forth a convincing argument or winning a contentious exchange of opinions, while the former could involve practically any means conceivable.

   Wrangle is also a synonym of the verb *struggle,* in contexts where the word *wrestle* would seem more appropriate. *Wangle* sometimes shows up in such contexts, but is generally not used in this way.

---

wrangle   **116**

Although Burr had eagerly joined the Revolutionary War in 1775 as a glory-seeking nineteen-year-old, his participation appears more personal than patriotic. He **wrangled** with Washington over inferiors' being promoted over him, and in 1779, after several threats to do so, he finally resigned his commission.

—Gordon S. Wood, *Revolutionary Characters*

The two great powers **wrangled** for influence over Persia through concessions and loans and other tools of economic diplomacy.

—Daniel Yergin, *The Prize: The Epic Quest for Oil, Money & Power*

When she learned that John Glenn had **wrangled** a return flight to space in order to study the aging body, she was finally prompted to return to America and campaign for her shot into space.

—Pamela Freni, *Space for Women: A History of Women with the Right Stuff*

In their best of times sheep go through life in a near-panic, and their frenzied bleating as they were **wrangled** up the chutes into boxcars grew to a storm of sound.

—Ivan Doig, *This House of Sky: Landscapes of a Western Mind*

Frenchy was a connector, one of the especially agile ironworkers whose task was to snatch steel from the sky as it came sailing in on the boom of the derrick, then **wrangle** it into the building's frame.

—Jim Rasenberger, "The 'Sky Boys,'" *New York Times*, April 3, 2006

The 100 Words

adherence
adhesion
adopted
adoptive
amend
baleful
baneful
beyond the pale
cache
cachet
condemn
congenital
contemn
contemptible
contemptuous
delegate
deprecate
depreciate
distinct
distinctive
emend
energize
enervate
exceptionable
exceptional
expedient
expeditious
faze
flounder
founder
free rein
gambit
gamut
gibe

gotten
gybe
historic
historical
hoard
horde
injustice
jibe[1]
jibe[2]
jibe[3]
jive
lend
load
loan
lode
majority
masterful
masterly
militate
mitigate
no holds barred
old
older
ordinance
ordnance
passed
past
peace
peremptory
phase
piece
plurality
pore
pour

practicable
practical
preemptive
rationale
rationalization
relegate
repress
restive
restless
shined
shone
sleight of hand
slew[1]
slew[2]
slew[3]
slough[1]
slough[2]
slue
suppress
tenant
tenet
throe
toe the line
unexceptionable
unexceptional
unjust
venal
venial
waive
wangle
wave
wrangle